OUTSIDERS

A YOHAN TYTLER MYSTERY

FAWAZ JALEEL

INSIDERS

VERSUS

OUTSIDERS

A YOHAN TYTLER MYSTERY

FAWAZ JALEEL

KALAMOS LITERARY SERVICES LLP

Kalamos Literary Services LLP
Email: info@kalamos.co.in
First Published in 2024
by
Kalamos Literary Services

ISBN – 978-81-19601-38-7

Insiders vs Outsiders
Fawaz Jaleel

Cover designed and typeset in Kalamos Literary Services LLP

Even when the world turns against you, there are some people who always have your back and join your fight, no matter how huge the challenge is. Cherish them.

This is a dedication…

To India, the inspiration for all my stories and the wonderful home it provides to me and a billion others.

To my parents, brother, friends, and relatives who have always stood by me.

My dearest Abhayan, you will forever hold a special place in our hearts. Without you, the best years of our lives would have been devoid of meaning.

To the readers who embraced Yohan #1 (Nobody Likes An Outsider). Thank you. Feel free to write to me at fawazjr@gmail.com to discuss stories.

The challenges for an Outsider to enter any industry are greater than for others. Just because it is more challenging doesn't mean it's impossible. Keep going, people.

Chapter 1
THE CHAOS BEGINS IN CALCUTTA

"As I walk through the alleys of Tiretta Bazaar in Calcutta, I see the market brimming with red and joy. Once home to over 20,000 Indian-Chinese nationals, today, the population may have fallen to well below 5,000, but the spirit of Chinese New Year remains as high as ever. I am about to end my night reporting on this cultural fiesta in Kolkata at one of the city's most famous Kathi roll vendors, Shoung Lee – a third-generation Indian-Chinese national who sells her ever-in-demand rolls made with her grandfather's secret chilli sauce. Every foodie wants a taste of this, and more than them, Shoung Lee has to protect the secret recipe from the thousands of competitors who have attempted to recreate this culinary magic repeatedly. With a delicious roll in my hand and our hungry-looking cameraperson Mithun Bose behind the lens, this is Adinarayan Mahendran reporting for News Now from Calcutta."

There was something about 44-year-old Adinarayan's reporting that gave life to the cities and their supposedly inanimate specialties. Adi always dressed according to the place's unique characteristic, wanting his news to tower above his tall, well-built personality, complemented by his strikingly long nose visible on his oval-shaped face, which always sported a five-day unshaven stubble.

"What a fine P2C, Adi da," Mithun quickly complimented and was even quicker to grab the Kathi roll he had been eyeing while Adi praised the city and the delicacy.

"Why do you use abbreviations, Mithun? At least let's use complete words while speaking," Adi forced his contempt for abbreviations and millennial lingo on the cameraperson, whom he had met just during this assignment. Even though P2C is a universally accepted journalistic slang that refers to a reporter's final one-on-one with the camera as they close a story, Adi preferred using full sentences.

Mithun, the freelancer, who was completely unaware of his reporter's finicky obsession, chose to ignore the comment and focus on his present - the sumptuous food in sight.

Shoung-Lee, who was busy tossing the whole flour bread base for the rolls, smiled at the unimportant problems of the reporter who covered her stall. However, being a true saleswoman, she tossed some extra chilli sauce onto Adi's plate, hoping to cheer him up.

After thanking Lee, the two-man crew of News Now proceeded to shoot more visuals of the cultural extravaganza that could be used for subsequent coverages or be occasional fillers when there wasn't abundant news.

The English calendar might record today as Friday, 12th February 2022, proving 42 days have ended since the new year started, but today marked the first day of the Chinese New Year. Across the world, Chinese nationals celebrate this sixteen-day festival with great joy and happiness. They exchange red packets or *ang baos* with money with their relatives, especially children, who look forward to these coveted presents. As per tradition, this was the 'Year of the Ox' based on the 12 zodiac signs representing each year. The year before was the 'Year of the Rat', and the Year that will follow will be the 'Year of the Tiger'.

"You know, it's funny that the Chinese New Year in 2020 was the year of the rat. It kind of makes sense. The whole world just stayed closed in their little holes the whole year," Mithun tried to bring a smile to Adi's face.

"That's a very insensitive thing to say, man. I think we shouldn't mock our neighbour's sentiments." Adi wasn't one of those people who rattled 'populist' jokes or stereotype-laden comments. Being a voracious reader, apart from working majorly as a crime-beat journalist, Adi had well-defined opinions on politics, culture, international relations and more. You wouldn't expect him to make a sexist remark or a cultural appropriation joke. Adi knew better and wanted people around him to think a little before they uttered meaningless words.

"Adi da. Tell me something. Why are you covering this festival? Usually, junior reporters are sent for this. You are a very experienced journalist. I have seen your crime reports. Big fan, sir." Mithun now resorted to singing praises garbed as questions to lighten up the senior reporter. You wouldn't judge him a lot if you put yourself in Mithun's shoes, though. Being a freelance reporter, he needed Adinarayan to sign off on this assignment's invoice, sanction fuel allowance, and secure a recommendation for future projects in the city. It doesn't take a genius to figure out Mithun's situation, and being a crime reporter for 23 years, the 44-year-old Adinarayan knew the intention behind Mithun's day-long quest to please him.

"Well, isn't it a good thing that a crime reporter is covering culture? Maybe fewer people are dying." Adi didn't mean what he said, nor did he want to reveal why he was forced to take up the assignment. However, he felt that it was necessary to acknowledge Mithun's efforts and go easy on him while also hiding the fact that he understood that the 'junior cameraperson' wanted to prepare for the coming Valentine's Day that would happen in two days while Adi had no such item on his agenda since he and his wife had an unusual marriage.

"True, true. Reporting on a cultural story is way better than doing a crime one." Now, Mithun wasn't even trying. He just wanted to agree and keep Adi in his suddenly better mood.

"Okay, Mithun. Don't worry about your bills. I'll file them as soon as I reach Delhi. Now, take me to the police station near my hotel. I need to file a complaint about my missing phone."

There was a sheepish smile on Mithun's face. It lit up like a sixty-watt bulb in a small, dark room. He quickly dusted off the semi-fried whole flour bread remains from the Kathi roll that stuck to his black cotton turtleneck, got up, patted off the dust on his beige chinos, and enthusiastically hopped onto his bike. Mithun found the perfect way to end his day and probably leave a good last impression on his client.

"The nearest police station to your hotel is Baguiati. I'll drive you there," Mithun said as he started his bike.

"Do you want me to hold your phone to help you navigate?" Adi offered to help.

"Adi da, we have been here since morning. My phone has given up, too. Anyway, I am a local boy. I know the way." Although laden with a heavy Bengali accent, Mithun spoke fine English until he asked Adi, *"Amara ekta prashna ache. Ratera khabara samparke ki, Adi da?"* Adi figured Mithun had dished out Bengali, but he was flustered at the timing and meaning and used the most 'unacceptable' yet 'acceptable' phrase in any language, *"Ami bhalo bangla bolte parina,"* which roughly evoked the same effect as '*Kannada gothilla*' or 'Hindi nahin maloom' or 'I don't know the language.'

"Haha. Sorry, sorry. I was thinking about the police station, and Bengali just came out naturally. I was just asking you about dinner," Mithun was quick to translate.

"Aah. We can eat something near my hotel. Not from it, though. Their dal makhani tasted unforgivable," Adi chuckled as he further expressed his desire to have some local cuisine.

Adinarayan was given a three-star hotel in Raghunathpur, a low-key residential area not far from the City Centre Mall—a stand-alone four-storeyed building with bare minimum facilities to secure the 3-star rating. A 2700 Rs per night accommodation was all that was allowed for the crime reporter with 23 years of experience. Then, again, a man who rarely stayed in his hotel out of choice or by the sheer demands of his profession, Adi didn't mind it. At quarter past nine, it was a refreshing ride through Calcutta's roads, albeit the final destination being a police station. Mithun, who knew the city well enough, could have taken the Dum Dum Road or the Ratan Road to the police station. But he knew something that Adi didn't. The famous Howrah Bridge was just 2 kilometres behind their current location, and a slight detour would be refreshing for the two of them. Playing on Adi's unfamiliarity with the place, Mithun did just that. As they reached the Howrah bridge, they were welcomed by its majestic green pillar, water on both sides and centrally-located double-headed street lamp posts that shone with colourful lighting. More importantly, the gentle breeze that gushed through their hair and gave them the smell and taste of Kolkata was most delightful. It was a beautiful ride sans the traffic, and Mithun rode quickly enough to make up for the time they were losing due to the detour. From the bridge, he took Dum Dum Road and continued letting Adinarayan embrace the warmth and gentleness of his city, which brimmed with culture and calm.

Around quarter to ten, they reached the Baguiati police station, and Mithun drove inside the premises to park his bike. Contrary to the police uniform in several parts of India, one could see officers dressed in white and white while yellow police vans were parked outside.

Mithun asked the guard if the inspector was around. As the guard spoke to Mithun, he couldn't help but stare at Adinarayan's face as though he had seen someone familiar. The veteran journalist noticed the stare and wondered if his crime reporting from Mumbai was as popular in the city of joy, too.

Mithun took the necessary permissions to meet the sub-inspector in charge, Aurobinda Das. As Mithun and Adi pushed open the door, the latter continued to notice more stares directed at him from the local police officials. Unaware of the attention his colleague was garnering, Mithun walked in and stood near the visitors' chairs behind Inspector Das' desk.

"*Shubho Shonda, ami ki apanake sahayya karate pari,*" the inspector was examining his file and did not look up to greet the visitors, but he seemed really friendly as he initiated the conversation by asking how he could help them.

Mithun figured it was important for the conversation to continue in English for Adi's benefit and requested the officer, *"Amara bandhu Bangla bolte pari na. Apni ingreji bolte paren?"*

Adi understood that perfectly well, as it was an extension of the single Bengali line he had used when Mithun had spoken to him earlier.

"Yes. Tell me, young man," the older Mr. Das acknowledged the request and finally looked at the two gentlemen in front of him.

"This is my senior colleague, Adinarayan, from News Now, Mumbai. He lost his mobile phone sometime today. He claims he didn't have it when he reached Tiretta bazaar, so he must have lost it in the morning before leaving, or somewhere in the taxi," Mithun explained the situation.

"It should be in the taxi because I had it when I left my hotel. Since it was a yellow taxi, I don't have the driver's details or the car's number, and my phone was switched off when we tried calling it."

As Adinarayan explained, a subordinate of Mr. Das entered the room with a file while staring at the seasoned journalist. Being a keen observer, Adi figured that the smile wasn't one of familiarity. The assistant sub-inspector's smile displayed more intrigue than acknowledgement, but there wasn't enough information for Adi to fathom the cause. The ASI opened the file and murmured something into his senior's ears.

"*Ore baba re*! How did I miss this?" Inspector Das was appalled at his memory.

"What happened, sir?" Adinarayan was curious.

"Well, Mr. Adinarayan Mahendran," Das added the surname that had not been revealed to him by the two visitors. "The Calcutta police have been on a manhunt for the last two hours. So I am afraid the case we have in hand right now is bigger than finding your missing mobile phone."

A slightly perturbed Adinarayan took out his handkerchief to wipe his sweaty palms and asked, "Who are you looking for, sir?"

"You. Mr. Adinarayan Mahendran."

***

Clothes, wallet, charger, iPad – Adinarayan quickly grabbed everything he could. He didn't have the time to patiently recheck multiple times like one would when they left a hotel room. Usually a neat packer, the journalist didn't have the time to arrange things as he would have wished. Downstairs, in the hotel driveway, Mithun waited with a taxi driver who would drive Adi to the Netaji Subhash Chandra Bose International Airport. Adi cancelled his tickets scheduled for the next day and rebooked himself on a flight that left in the next two and a half hours.

Despite the glaring insufficiencies, the reception desk bucked up and ensured their tense guest had a smooth check-out, thanks to Mithun's persuasive push.

Outside the hotel lobby, Mithun rushed up the five small stairs, quickly grabbed Adi's suitcase, and placed it in the front seat, next to the driver.

"Adi da. I don't know what to say… I… I wish I could do something," Mithun struggled for words. Adi adjusted his moist, due to perspiration, spectacle frames and placed his right hand on Mithun's left shoulder, expressing gratitude to the young cameraperson. Mithun had a lot more to say, but he just didn't have enough words to convey it. Adi entered the car and instructed the driver to rush to the airport. Since the airport was less than five kilometres away and the Bangaon-Kulpi Road had no traffic, they would reach their destination in less than ten minutes.

Just ten minutes… but that was enough for Adinarayan to recollect his conversation with Inspector Aurobinda Das.

"Mr. Adinarayan, it's always difficult to convey such news…" the senior sub-inspector started.

"What happened, sir?" Adi hated it when people strayed with words, and the tension was already eating his mental peace.

"There was a fire at your apartment complex in Mumbai. Apparently, a party of some sort was happening on the same floor, and all we know is that around fourteen people died, including your wife. Your colleagues have been trying to reach you since evening, and your phone, as well as your colleague's, was switched off. I am really sorry for your loss," Das had the knack of a veteran with ample experience in conveying such terrible, unwelcome news to close aides of victims.

A journalist, a crime beat one at that, Adinarayan knew what was coming. His parents had passed away much earlier, and his wife and sister were the only remaining family. His sister stayed in Delhi, and the moment Inspector Das mentioned Mumbai, the outcome was more or less clear in Adi's mind. It wasn't the smoothest of marriages for Adinarayan and his literary agent wife, Mekhala Thambi. Originally from Kerala, the two were children of second-generation Mumbai Malayalees whose parents met each other via a matrimonial app with specific filters, including religion, caste, complexion, wealth, and so forth. The couple had drifted apart over the years for several reasons, but news of this nature would crumble any man. For Adi, the 34-year-old Mekhala might have just been a 'socially documented' roommate masquerading as a wife, but her presence in the house ensured he didn't have to return to an empty house. Even amidst the hardships of a drifting marriage, there was a sense of companionship. They were there for each other, albeit the situations being few and far between — sometimes in terms of mere presence when one needed it, and at other times as a confidant during trying moments. The relationship was basic, almost as if they were simply fulfilling the obligations of a marriage contract – Adi and Mekhala had that going for them.

He may not have been in love with her, but the news of her demise had him in tears. He wasn't an expressive man, and hence, there wasn't any breakdown. It was not behaviour induced by the unrealistic expectations of toxic masculinity because Adi wasn't 'that man', but he generally didn't know how to express himself anymore. Perhaps it was something his parents would be crying in their graves for.

The taxi dropped him at the entrance, and Adi quickly paid the driver and grabbed his cabin baggage from the front seat. As he frantically searched for the right entrance gate for his Indigo flight, there was a pat on his back. He turned around, and to his surprise, Mithun stood in front of him.

"I just thought I'd come to the airport and say goodbye and take care." This wasn't Mithun trying to get his bills cleared. It was genuine compassion as he was the only person who knew Adi's situation.

"Thanks, brother. This means an awful lot. You really didn't have to come, but…" Adi did not complete the sentence and went on to hug Mithun. His mind was still processing the unwelcome news, and he had no idea what it would be like to return to that house where he would probably have to live alone for the rest of his life. Adi may not have been in love with his wife, but her sheer presence helped him deal with his anxieties and live a satisfactory life.

With a heavy heart and a teary-eyed goodbye, the man trudged towards the airport entrance, dragging his suitcase as he went. Inside the Netaji Subhash Chandra Bose International Airport, he was greeted by a strangely half-empty terminal. The silence was almost palpable, broken only by the sound of his footsteps echoing against the walls.

As he made his way towards the check-in counter, he felt his emotions welling up. A lone tear rolled down his cheek, a testament to the sadness he was feeling. Suddenly, he noticed a crowd gathering around a common television screen nearby. Curiosity piqued, he completed his check-in process and joined the throng. As he approached, he could hear snippets of the breaking news, and his heart began to race.

As he reached the edge of the crowd, his eyes widened and he began to sweat profusely. The news that was being broadcast was nothing short of shocking, and Adi was unable to tear his eyes away from the screen.

The opposition leader, Kailash Mukherjee, was a man who never shied away from using his voice to make an impact. His speeches were a spectacle to behold, filled with fiery rhetoric and accusations that echoed through the screens and reverberated in the hearts of his followers. Even though he was just a two-dimensional figure on the television screen, his chest-thumping antics could be felt as if he were standing right there in the room.

The television anchor looked sceptical as Kailash Mukherjee ranted about the Prime Minister's involvement in Mekhala Thampi's murder.

"Mr. Mukherjee, what evidence do you have to support your claims?" the anchor asked with conviction.

"I don't need evidence to know the truth," Kailash replied, his voice rising with indignation. "I have sources, sources that go deep into the heart of the ruling party. And they have told me that Mekhala Thampi was silenced because she was representing a book that exposed a mining scam involving the Prime Minister himself."

"But Mr. Mukherjee, isn't it irresponsible to make such serious accusations without concrete evidence?" the anchor pressed.

"Irresponsible?" Kailash scoffed. "I have been in this game longer than you've been alive, son. I know how things work. And mark my words, the truth will come out. And when it does, those who tried to silence me will regret it."

The anchor could tell that Kailash was not going to budge from his narrative. He was convinced of his own righteousness, and no amount of scepticism would change his mind.

"Thank you for your time, Mr. Mukherjee. We'll be following this story closely," the anchor said, trying to wrap up the interview.

"Follow it all you want, my boy. But mark my words, the truth will come out. And when it does, those who tried to silence me will regret it," Kailash said, his eyes blazing with conviction.

Adinarayan sat in the airport, lost in thought. He couldn't shake off the unsettling feeling that lingered within him after seeing the heated interview with Kailash Mukherjee. His mind was clouded with thoughts of his late wife, and the accusations made by the opposition leader only served to intensify his grief.

As he looked around the airport, Adinarayan couldn't help but overhear the chatter of the other passengers around him. The news of his wife's murder and the accusations made by Mukherjee had spread like wildfire, and everyone seemed to have an opinion on the matter.

Despite being the husband of the murdered Mekhala, Adinarayan found himself struggling to dismiss the public's scepticism towards Mukherjee's claims. He knew that Kailash was a pompous politician who would do anything to gain political mileage, but at the same time, he couldn't help but wonder if there was any truth to the allegations.

Adinarayan took a deep breath and tried to compose himself. He knew that he couldn't let his emotions get in the way of his work. He had to remain objective and impartial in his reporting, even if it meant delving into painful memories.

As he waited for his flight to Mumbai, Adinarayan's mind was filled with questions. What evidence did Mukherjee have to support his claims? Could a book really have led to Mekhala Thampi's murder? Was there any truth to the allegations levied against the Prime Minister?

Despite his grief, Adinarayan was determined to get to the bottom of this story and uncover the truth. He knew that it was his duty as a journalist to report the facts, no matter how difficult they may be. As he waited for his flight, Adinarayan resolved to do whatever it took to get justice for his late wife and bring the truth to light.

Chapter 2
ALL'S NOT WELL IN MUMBAI

Adinarayan stared at the burnt remains of his 2-bedroom apartment, feeling a mix of emotions. His late wife, Mekhala Thampi, may not have been his beloved wife, nor were they close. They had married under parental pressure, and while they had tried to make it work, their marriage had never been a happy one. Despite this, the news of Mekhala's death had hit him hard. She may not have been his soulmate, but she was still a human being, and the fact that she had died in such a horrific way was difficult to process.

Adinarayan walked around the apartment, taking in the destruction around him. The kitchen, where the fire had spread from the other flat, was unrecognisable. The walls were charred, and the appliances had melted due to the intense heat. The living room, adjacent to the kitchen, was a mess, with furniture burnt to a crisp. The bedroom was the only place that seemed relatively untouched, but the smoke damage was evident even there.

Adinarayan couldn't help but think about his neighbours as he walked around. His neighbours were a Bengali couple and had a teenage son who loved to throw parties. Adinarayan and Mekhala had never really gotten to know them, but they had heard the noise and commotion coming from their apartment on numerous occasions.

The police report stated that the fire had started in the neighbour's apartment, likely due to a faulty electrical outlet that had been overloaded with party equipment. Thirteen of the fourteen people who died in the fire were in that apartment, while Adinarayan's wife became a casualty at her own house.

As he stood in the ruins of his former home, Adinarayan felt a sense of anger and frustration. He couldn't believe that such a tragedy had transpired because of someone else's negligence. The fact that his neighbours' party had been the cause of the fire only added to his anger.

But deep down, he knew that there was no use in dwelling on the past. The damage had been done, and no amount of anger or frustration would change that. All he could do now was pick up the pieces of his shattered life and move forward.

As he took a deep breath and tried to focus on the future, Adinarayan knew that it wouldn't be easy. He was sitting in the burnt-down living room, lost in thought when suddenly the doorbell rang. He made his way to the door and opened it to find Circle Inspector Siad Kamble of the Andheri East station standing there. As a known face on television, Adinarayan was used to being recognised, but he found it unsettling that Siad addressed him as 'Adi' as if he already knew him. Nevertheless, his mind was in a different space, hit hard by the death of Mekhala.

"Good evening, Adi. How are you holding up?" Siad asked as he stepped inside.

Adinarayan sighed and replied, "I'm still coping, Inspector. It's been tough."

Siad nodded sympathetically and began to look around the apartment. He walked towards the burnt kitchen remains and surveyed the area. "It's a terrible tragedy. I'm sorry for your loss," he said.

Adinarayan nodded, and Siad asked, "So, Adi, can you tell me where you went and why?"

Adinarayan responded, "I was asked to go to Calcutta by my news agency. I was covering for a colleague."

Siad sighed and said, "Look, Adi, I'll be honest with you. This case clearly appears to be an accident; we're just following protocol by investigating it thoroughly. But the opposition leader has made it an issue because your wife recently met with the Prime Minister. They're using it as a political tool, you see."

Adinarayan felt a twinge of anger rise in him. He didn't want his wife's death to be turned into a political issue, but he knew that he was powerless to stop it. "I see," he said, trying to keep his tone neutral.

Siad continued, "I just wanted to let you know that we're doing everything we can to get to the bottom of this. We'll keep you updated on any developments."

Adinarayan nodded, feeling a mix of frustration and resignation. He knew that the political climate in the country was always volatile, and he couldn't help but feel that his wife's death was being used as a pawn in a larger game.

"Can you tell me a little more about your wife's job, Adi?" Siad asked.

Adinarayan replied, "She was a literary agent and worked with top publishing houses. She even represented some of India's crème de la crème, including sportspersons, business people, and politicians."

Adinarayan thought back to how he had never really asked his wife much about her job and realised that he only knew so much. He couldn't help but feel a sense of regret for not showing more interest in her work.

Siad looked around the burnt remains of the house as he prepared to leave. He and his constable walked around, hoping to find any information that could help them better understand Mrs. Thampi. Among the ashes and debris in the living room lay a few photos. Siad browsed through them and saw that apart from a wedding photo, there were just individual pictures of Adinarayan and his wife. The slightly stocky 42-year-old Inspector found it odd that there were no group pictures with friends or family.

But he decided not to press Adinarayan on this matter and asked him to visit the station to complete some formalities before he left. "Adi, you will have to come to the station tomorrow to complete the formalities. We need a statement from you, and we also need to take a look at your wife's laptop and mobile phone. It's just a formality, you understand," Siad said, trying to sound reassuring.

Adinarayan nodded, still lost in his own thoughts. "Yes, yes, I will come," he replied absentmindedly.

As Siad and his constable made their way out of the building, Adinarayan was left alone in the silence of his burnt apartment, surrounded by the memories of his late wife.

****

As Adinarayan reached the Andheri East police station to complete the formalities, several police constables who had seen him on television rushed to welcome him and take him inside. They seated him in the Circle Inspector's room, and in the absence of the CI, the constables brought the paperwork to Adinarayan.

Adinarayan sat in the Circle Inspector's room, feeling a sense of unease. The room was small and stuffy, with yellowed walls and a flickering fluorescent light that added to the gloom. The air was thick with the smell of stale cigarette smoke and old papers. Adinarayan looked around, feeling a sense of claustrophobia.

Adinarayan barely acknowledged them. He was lost in his thoughts, still trying to come to terms with the tragedy that had befallen him. Satish, the Head Constable, could sense that Adinarayan was in no state to talk, so he decided to leave him alone for a while.

"Please, fill out these forms, sir," Satish said, placing the paperwork in front of Adinarayan. "We need these details for our records."

Adinarayan nodded and started filling out the forms. Satish stood by, watching him as he worked. The room was silent except for the scratching of the pen on paper. After a few minutes, Adinarayan handed the forms back to Satish.

Adinarayan's gaze was blank when he received the paperwork from the police. As a senior journalist, he couldn't help but peruse it even in his weakened state of mind. As he skimmed through the post-mortem report, a few words caught his attention, and his eyes widened in surprise.

The report stated, *Gas chromatography-mass spectrometry (GC-MS) analysis of Mekhala's blood samples revealed the presence of propane and butane gases. The concentration of these gases in her blood was alarming, at 46.6 mg/dL and 23.8 mg/dL, respectively.*

Adinarayan removed his spectacles, rubbing his eyes to ensure he wasn't reading it wrong. His investigative instincts kicked in, and despite the overwhelming sorrow he felt, his mind sharpened, and he began to connect the dots. He had seen this before, and he knew exactly what it meant.

"Satish ji," Adinarayan spoke up suddenly, "wasn't a faulty electrical connection in the neighbour's apartment the cause of the fire?"

The Head Constable nodded, a little taken aback by Adinarayan's sudden outburst. "Yes, Adinarayan sir," he replied, wondering where the conversation was headed.

"Look at this report," Adi said, pointing to the words that had caught his eye. "What do you make of it?"

The Head Constable, who was nearing his retirement, looked dumbfounded. He struggled to understand the journalist's angle and stammered out a reply.

"I... I'm not sure, sir. Perhaps it's best to discuss it with the Circle Inspector," he said, gesturing towards the door. "Let me go and call him."

Adinarayan nodded, lost in the paperwork, as the Head Constable scurried out of the room. He couldn't shake off the feeling that something was amiss. He continued to browse through the reports, hoping to find something that would help him connect the dots. He took out his new phone he had just bought and started taking pictures of the reports for future reference.

The police officials in the room were partly in awe of the senior journalist and unsure how to respond to his inquiries. They stood around awkwardly, watching him take copies of the official records. After a few minutes, the Head Constable returned to the room, followed by the Circle Inspector, Siad Kamble.

Siad greeted Adinarayan with a warm smile, but his expression quickly turned serious. "Hello, Adi sir. Satish ji said you have some concerns?" he asked, gesturing for Adinarayan to take a seat.

Adinarayan took a deep breath and began, "The post-mortem report says that there was an excessive presence of propane and butane in my wife's body." He paused, his eyes fixed on Siad's face, waiting for a reaction.

The CI's cabin was quiet except for the rhythmic ticking of the wall clock. Siad finally spoke up, "Mekhala ji must have been cooking or something when the fire started, and it must have been fatal."

Adinarayan wasn't satisfied with this explanation. "Let's assume you're right. Even if that was the case, this is still an excessive amount of gas in the body of a person who was cooking."

Siad's brows furrowed, "What are you trying to say, sir?"

Adinarayan leaned forward, his eyes locked on Siad's, "This happened due to a gas leak, and it must have been leaking for quite some time."

Siad opened his mouth to speak, but Adinarayan cut him off, "My wife never used the kitchen. She didn't know how to cook at all. I am the only one who cooked in the house."

Siad's eyes widened in surprise. "What, sir? *Ladies log* know cooking."

Adinarayan's face twisted with disgust at the CI's sexist remark. "Siad sir, please make more responsible comments. A woman doesn't need to know how to cook. It's not a rule." However, what was even more concerning for him was the CI's inability to process the information. It was as if Siad was unable to see the significance of the excessive amount of gas found in Mekhala's body, and Adinarayan couldn't help but feel frustrated by his lack of understanding.

Siad's eyes flicked nervously to Adinarayan's face. The journalist's piercing gaze seemed to bore into him, and Siad felt a knot form in his stomach. He knew that Adinarayan had a reputation for exposing the truth, no matter how uncomfortable it might be, and he feared that the journalist might use this information to bring down the entire department.

"Adi sir. What are you trying to say?" Siad asked, his voice quivering slightly. He couldn't help but feel that the journalist was on to something and was worried about what that might mean for his job and reputation.

"Siad sir," Adinarayan's voice rose, "what I am saying is that there has to be a reason why there was a gas leak in the house, especially when Mekhala never touched the stove."

Siad tried to suggest, "No cook also, sir?"

"Of course not, Siad. I would have told you if that possibility existed," Adi replied firmly.

Siad looked helpless and asked, "What should I do, sir?"

Adinarayan's investigative instincts had kicked in, and he declared, "I want the post-mortem reports of the neighbours and the guests."

Siad hesitated, "But sir… that is confidential."

"Siad, I need to see it. What if you are missing something?" Adi persisted, his eyes narrowing.

The Circle Inspector reluctantly agreed and gestured to his Head Constable to bring in the files. Adinarayan's mind raced with the possibilities as he waited for the reports, wondering what they could be.

Adinarayan meticulously sifted through the post-mortem reports of the thirteen other deceased individuals, his eyes scanning each word with intense scrutiny. As he read the report of the neighbour Mr, Bhattacharya, his brows furrowed with increasing suspicion.

The investigation revealed that the fire was caused by faulty electrical wiring in the building. The electrical wiring ignited nearby combustible materials, and upon internal examination, the chest cavity was opened to reveal that his lungs were congested with carbon particles, indicating that the victim was breathing carbon monoxide present in smoke during the fire. The internal organs were charred, and the peritoneum and pleura were also burnt…

The reports were eerily similar—all of them had succumbed to carbon monoxide poisoning due to the same faulty electrical wiring that had caused the fatal fire in Adinarayan's home.

The journalist was verifying the statements one by one, his mind racing with the implications of what he was uncovering.

His eyes widened with each passing report. "Siad ji. Were there any signs of forced entry to my house in the hours leading up to the fire?" Adinarayan's voice was low and urgent, and his investigative instincts pushed him to delve deeper.

"As I told you, sir, this is a routine fire case. I understand that you're going through a tough time, but please don't blow up an open and shut case," Siad said, maintaining his stance.

"If that's the case, why were there traces of propane and butane just in my wife's body when there's no chance that she would leave the gas on?" Adinarayan persisted, his voice rising with each word.

"It could have been anything," Siad replied defensively.

Adinarayan's eyes narrowed, his voice low and menacing. "Anything? Do you know how improbable that sounds? My wife, who was so careful and meticulous, suddenly decided to leave the gas on. No, Siad, something else is going on here, and I intend to find out what it is."

Siad shifted uneasily in his seat, feeling the weight of Adinarayan's intense gaze on him. He knew the journalist was right. Something wasn't adding up, and he was starting to regret dismissing Adinarayan's concerns so quickly.

But before he could say anything, Adinarayan beat him to it, "I want to see the security footage from the night of the fire. And I want it now."

Siad hesitated, knowing that the footage was confidential and only accessible to the police. But the look in Adinarayan's eyes was enough to make him cave. With a resigned sigh, he picked up the phone and called the Evidence Bureau.

Adinarayan impatiently tapped his foot, his heart racing with anticipation. Sweat dripped down his forehead as he watched Circle Inspector Siad pace back and forth, his voice hushed as he spoke into the phone. Adi could feel the tension building with each passing moment.

Finally, Siad hung up the phone and approached Adi with a look of frustration etched on his face. "Adi, there's a problem," he began, scratching his head nervously.

Adi's patience was wearing thin. "Now what?" he demanded.

Siad hesitated before replying, "I'm afraid this is beyond my jurisdiction. We may need to involve higher authorities."

Adi's heart sank. The gravity of the situation was written all over Siad's face. Something seemed amiss as the CI appeared evasive with his answers.

"What's happening, Siad?" he asked.

"Apparently, the Central Government has handed over the case to the CBI."

Siad's response not only confused Adinarayan but also the police officials in the room.

"The CBI? Why would they be asked to investigate a routine fire accident?" Adinarayan asked, his voice shaky with emotion.

Siad nodded grimly, "I think it's due to the pressure exerted by the opposition leader. The government wants to rule out any instance of foul play."

"Why does the opposition leader care about a fire accident in my house?" Adinarayan's mind was racing with questions.

Siad shrugged, "Maybe they see an opportunity to exploit the situation for political gain. Either way, we are now out of the picture."

Adinarayan clenched his fists, feeling a sense of helplessness wash over him.

"One thing is clear from the reports. My wife's death wasn't an accident. It looks like a well-planned murder," Adinarayan finally voiced his biggest fear and revelation. "Just that somebody higher up figured this out before we did."

Siad tried to process the gravity of the journalist's claim. Adinarayan's eyes blazed with anger as he thought about the unknown enemy who had orchestrated his wife's murder.

"Do you, by any chance, know who the investigating officer is?" Adi asked, curious.

Siad's face turned pale. "Yes, they mentioned a name... Tytler... something."

Adinarayan's eyes lit up but with a sense of unease he asked, "Yohan Tytler?"

Chapter 3
IT'S JUST THE BEGINNING

CBI Headquarters
Delhi

In an area that emanates the scent of power and reeks of secrecy, just below the Jangpura bridge, lies the prominent Central Government complex–CGO complex–the headquarters of the Central Bureau of Investigation. Overlooking the Ministry of Electronics & Information Technology, the physical structure symbolises the confidentiality and discretion that characterises the nature of the work of the people there. The building, made entirely of glass, hides the view inside, rendering the building more mysterious.

CBI Director Jagat Verma sat in his spacious cabin, perusing a few documents and performing his official duties. Suddenly, there was a polite knock on his door.

"May I come in, sir?" the young officer asked respectfully.

"Yes, yes. Yohan. Come in, son," Verma welcomed the young CBI officer with the affectionate demeanour of a father. Yohan had been steadily rising through the ranks of the organisation, earning accolades for his brilliant work.

"How are you, sir?" Yohan asked his boss, showing respect.

"I am fine. So, the Bihar chapter is done. Now it's Mumbai for you and your team," Verma referred to Yohan's previous case, where he had solved the murder of Ashraf Zain under volatile circumstances, making him a darling of the media and the masses. "Of course, the Home Minister spoke to you... so you are aware of the case, right?"

"Yes, sir. In fact, I have been reading through the case files. The local police seem to believe it's a regular fire accident." The young 32-year-old Yohan jumped quickly into action, showing confidence from having cracked his previous and first case as the lead investigator.

"What are your thoughts?" Jagat questioned.

"Sir, at the outset, it does look like an open-and-shut case. But the sheer fact that the Home Minister has called and asked me to investigate means that something doesn't add up," Yohan answered, reminding Director Verma of the call he had received in Bihar immediately after the previous case.

"Anything you have gathered so far that backs up these claims?" Jagat continued to probe.

"Actually, Mekhala Thampi does look like someone who could have made a few powerful enemies," Yohan replied.

"Really? A literary agent? A lady who kept herself in a world of books, can have such powerful enemies?" Verma was indulging in banter to gauge his officer's thought process.

"She has represented books of several people, including police officers, businessmen and even human rights activists. The books that have been released have been surrounded by multiple controversies. There could be several motives," Yohan explained elaborating on his investigation so far.

Jagat nodded, encouraging Yohan to continue.

"But there is something unusual, sir. The initial forensic investigation showed that someone had entered the house," Yohan stated.

"That could be anybody, a house help or someone who had access to the house," Verma replied.

"But, sir," Yohan continued, "Sukumar has been in touch with his local sources in the police. They informed us that Mekhala had no house help, and according to the security records, there were no guests either. This information makes the situation even more unusual, don't you think?"

Jagat Verma sat up and took notice of Yohan's observation. "What else did our man, Sukumar, discover?" he asked, his interest piqued. Verma always smiled when he mentioned Sukumar's name, as the man was one of the most peculiar characters he had encountered in all his years of work. Eccentric, but with the analytical prowess of an AI system, Sukumar never let any data slide by him. Verma had thoughtfully picked Yohan's team for the previous case and felt that Sukumar and Yohan had perfectly complementary skills, both with a penchant for data.

"So you and Sukumar are still going strong as a team, huh?" Verma chided.

"Haha, without *anna*, what will I do, sir?" Yohan replied with a smile.

"So you want your same team, right?" Verma confirmed.

"Absolutely. Ila Qureshi and Sukumar Azhagu, sir," Yohan replied with a punch in his voice.

"So, coming back to the case. Do you think it was someone from within the building behind Mekhala's death?" Verma quickly shifted gears.

"There were no signs of physical struggle or attack on Mekhala. So then, why did the person enter the house?" Yohan mused.

"Maybe it was just someone she knew from the building itself," Verma suggested.

"Possible. But it's also possible that the person arrived as a guest at some other place and then went to Mekhala's house," Yohan replied, calculating the probabilities in his head.

"Hmmm. Yohan, the Home Minister is closely following this, and I want no mistakes," Verma warned.

Verma's cautionary tone made it clear that this was a high-stakes case. Yohan nodded in agreement. He was fully aware of the importance of this investigation and the need for precision. Suddenly, his phone rang, and he quickly sought permission from Mr. Verma before answering the call.

"Yes, Ila, tell me," Yohan spoke into the phone, his tone attentive. He listened patiently as his officer spoke, and then his voice grew louder, causing concern to flicker across Verma's face.

"All okay, Yohan?" Verma asked, checking on his officer.

"It was Ila. We may have our first breakthrough in the Mekhala Thampi case. I must go," Yohan responded urgently, his mind already racing ahead to the next step in the investigation.

****

Ila and Sukumar sat in Yohan's new cabin, surrounded by files and case facts. Yohan's desk clearly reflected his personality – organised, systematic, and sophisticated. The wooden desk was adorned with an array of books ranging from Criminal Psychology to Indian History and Politics. Some notable books on his desk were, 'Criminal Minds' by John Douglas, 'India after Gandhi' by Ramachandra Guha and 'The Argumentative Indian' by Amartya Sen.

In the centre of his desk sat a collection of fountain pens—Yohan's prized possession. Most of the pens were gifts from his industrialist father as a reward for his academic accomplishments and comprised brands like Montblanc, Parker and Sheaffer.

The files on his table were neatly arranged in order of priority. Ila appreciated the fact that Yohan was so organised, but the only thing she hated was the lingering cigarette smell that came from the numerous Marlboro Lights cigarettes Yohan smoked. The ashtray on one corner of his desk was a constant reminder of his bad habit.

On the other hand, Sukumar was drawn to Yohan's perfume collection, which was kept on the right side of his office. The fragrance of the perfumes was an unusual contrast to the cigarette smoke. Yohan had a penchant for expensive perfumes and had a collection of some of the most exotic scents. A collection of blazers, each meticulously tailored in Jaipur, decked the shelves of his office. Although the blazers were of different colours, all of them had a similar cut, which accentuated Yohan's body frame.

Yohan turned his attention to his associate and Sub-Inspector Ila Qureshi, a woman with a calm exterior but a bundle of insurgency inside her mind owing to the multiple struggles in her personal life. "So tell me, Ila. What are your preliminary findings?" he asked.

"Yeah," Ila began, "Yohan, the faulty wiring was said to be the reason behind the fire, but–"

There was an unusual sense of silence due to abated breaths as Ila spoke and both Sukumar and Yohan eagerly waited to hear her findings.

"–the apartment's facility manager confirmed to me via call that the wiring inside the neighbour's house was checked when they had raised a complaint about a faulty appliance a few weeks ago," she stated.

"Are you saying that the wiring had no issue, Ila?" Sukumar appeared curious.

"Yes, Sukumar *anna.* Everything about this case seems fishy," Ila added to her observations.

"I agree," Sukumar nodded enthusiastically as he carefully adjusted his spectacles and hand-combed his curly hair. "See, my sources in the station said that Mekhala's husband has also raised suspicions about the entire episode. The post-mortem report shows the presence of cooking gas in Mekhala's body, whereas none of the other victims had it in their bodies."

"Why is that unusual, *anna*?" Ila was now intrigued.

"Because according to her husband, Mekhala never used the gas as she never cooked, but the amount of gas in her body clearly suggests a leak," Sukumar concluded.

"And there was also a sign of external entry. You folks are absolutely right; things don't add up," Yohan said as he turned around to add the case pointers on his large whiteboard that was hung against the wall. "So, this is not an open and shut case after all!"

"What do you guys think?" Sukumar looked at his colleagues.

"It appears we are going to investigate another murder, *anna.* You and I versus the world of crime," Yohan playfully packaged something so serious under the guise of humour to tease Sukumar.

"What, Yohan Sir?" Sukumar wasn't too happy, "We just came from Bihar. Let me spend some time with my wife also, *na*," he chided.

"Get her along with you to Mumbai, and you can go to Marine Drive for a nice long walk," Yohan kept the banter on.

"What, sir. Showing us dreams also that are middle-class. At least you could have offered a stay at the Taj Palace," Sukumar wasn't willing to give up.

Ila was enjoying the banter, having found that her comfort levels with the two officers had increased after their Bihar investigation. "Guys, if you are done with this bromance, can we continue with the investigation?" she confirmed.

Yohan nodded in agreement and asked her what her next steps were in investigating the case.

"I'm preparing a list of Mekhala's clients," Ila replied. "She had very interesting clientele, including some of the biggest names in India. I've also found books on her portfolio written by journalists, especially whistleblowers who have exposed various scams in different sectors like politics, sports and business."

"I am still trying to source that information, but I did come across a news article about Mekhala representing a banking journalist. Apparently, this journalist was about to reveal the name of a big business tycoon who had taken a large sum of money from a public bank and had defaulted on several payments."

Yohan's eyes widened at the revelation. "Do you have any indication of who this business tycoon could be?" he asked.

"I ran a quick check, and it seemed it could be one of two people. Either a diamond merchant based in Indore or an education business tycoon with multiple colleges and coaching institutes across Kota, Mumbai, Delhi, and more," Ila nodded.

Sukumar interrupted, "Guys, our flight tickets to Mumbai are booked for tonight. Can we wrap this up?"

Yohan nodded and said, "Let's get moving then. Ila, continue your investigation on the client list and any possible threats to Mekhala. Sukumar, see if you can find any leads on the two possible suspects. And let's reconvene at the hotel tonight to discuss our findings."

*****

Yohan, Ila, and Sukumar gathered in the lobby of their three-star hotel in the suburbs of Mumbai near the airport in Vile Parle. The lobby was sparsely decorated with dim lights, comfortable sofas, and a few chandeliers hanging from the ceiling. Despite the limited facilities, the hotel was well-maintained and had a peaceful ambience.

After completing their check-in formalities and freshening up, the trio gathered at their hotel lobby. Sukumar started the conversation with a grin, "Yohan, I must admit, I am surprised you slept through the flight. Your snoring could wake up the dead."

Yohan rolled his eyes and retorted, "Oh please, Sukumar, you were the one snoring like a freight train. The air hostess even came with a set of cotton buds to stuff your nose."

"Oh, so you were using me as an excuse to talk to the air hostess?" Sukumar chuckled.

"Well, you are the most unaware yet efficient wingman ever," Yohan laughed. "Anyway, Ila, any educated guesses on who could be the businessman her client was going to expose?"

Ila leaned forward and said, "Guys, I'm still on it, but there's something else I found that I forgot to mention earlier. It doesn't look like anything serious, though."

Sukumar interrupted, "Ila, you're on a roll. Leave something for me to investigate, too!"

"What did you find, Ila?" Yohan asked.

"I noticed that Mekhala used to make a lot of trips to Delhi. A lot, like at least 20 days in a month, were spent in Delhi, which seemed like a lot to me," Ila replied.

Sukumar added, "A lot of publishers are based in Delhi; it could be because of that."

Yohan interrupted, "While that is true, an agent spends a lot of time reading and bettering manuscripts, and submissions can be made online. Why physically visit, especially when neither the publisher nor the author pays for it?"

"I considered that angle," Ila said.

"Can you cross-check with the publishing houses about Mekhala's visits based on her travel dates?" Yohan asked.

"I already did," Ila replied.

"I can do a detailed analysis on when she booked the tickets, mode of payment, the timeline before which she booked, the costs, etc.," Sukumar said.

Yohan nodded, "That makes sense. *Anna*, see if you can identify any patterns?"

As they discussed Mekhala's trips to Delhi, Ila grew increasingly fidgety, tapping her foot and wringing her hands. Yohan, ever observant, noticed her behaviour and asked, "What's bothering you, Ila?"

Ila took a deep breath and said, "Well, based on my preliminary observation, Mekhala works with two of the most reputed Indian publishers, and both their offices are in Gurgaon. But Mekhala stays in Central Delhi, which is far and unsuitable for travelling daily to these publishing houses, especially since she spends more than 20 days there."

Yohan raised his eyebrows, lost in thought. "Ila, you create a journey chart based on Mekhala's activities. And *anna*, like I said, see if you can identify any patterns or regularities in her travels."

Ila nodded, her fingers already flying over the keyboard. "Sure, I can do that. It might take me a little while, though."

Suddenly, Yohan's eyes lit up as if a thought had just occurred to him. "Wait a minute, I remember seeing Mekhala's file. She's been a literary agent since 2016, but she was a corporate professional before that. Ila, check if these trips to Delhi were happening before she became a literary agent, too."

Ila paused typing and looked at Yohan curiously, "Why does that matter?"

"It might give us a clue on why she was making these trips," Yohan said, his eyes still sparkling with the excitement of a potential breakthrough.

Ila quickly delved into the case files and information she had gathered, her eyes scanning over the screen while she kept muttering to herself. "There are instances of Mekhala travelling to Delhi before 2015, too," she finally said.

"Interesting. So these trips might have something to do with her previous job. We need to dig deeper into her corporate background and see if there's a connection," Yohan nodded thoughtfully.

"I'll take that up, Yohan," Sukumar volunteered, "… so what is our plan of action for tomorrow?"

"Let's visit the police station and get a lowdown of their investigation. Expect some resistance, but that's okay," Yohan started briefing them. "After that, we'll go to Mekhala's house and try to talk to her husband, too."

Sukumar nodded in agreement and said, "Sounds good to me. Let's do it."

Yohan then turned to Ila and instructed her to find information on who had gone and repaired the faulty wiring in Mekhala's house.

"But what's your angle, Yohan?" Ila asked.

"It's too early to say anything for sure," Yohan replied, "... but the fact that it was repaired, and there are signs of an external entry, makes me suspicious."

Ila countered, "That could be a coincidence, though."

"Coincidences are a murderer's biggest gifts," Sukumar interjected. "By the way, do you know who Mekhala Thampi's husband is?"

Yohan nodded without making any further comments, but his mumble didn't sound too natural to his confidante.

"Why such a cold response? At least we are meeting a celebrity journalist tomorrow," Sukumar tried to whip up some enthusiasm.

"Well, I'm not too sure about that," Yohan's mumble was just a wee bit louder.

Ila's curiosity was piqued, and she shot back, "C'mon, boss, tell us."

"Well, he and I have history. I don't have a good feeling about this meeting," Yohan replied hesitantly.

Chapter 4
A BAD INVESTIGATOR ALWAYS BLAMES HIS CASE

Yohan and his team sat in the Toyota Innova as they made their way through the bustling streets of Mumbai. They were headed from their hotel in Vile Parle to Andheri East, where they were meeting the local police force. The city was alive with energy, and Yohan couldn't help but admire the wide Eastern Express Highway they were on, flanked by hoardings that primarily constituted cinema, politics, sports, and corporates—all the extremely prominent forces in the city.

As they drove, Yohan took out his phone and sent a text message to his father. *Pa, your past keeps coming in the way of my work.* He sighed and leaned back in his seat, lost in thought.

Despite the traffic, Mumbai was a city that had a certain charm to it. It was a melting pot of cultures and a hub for business, yet it had a distinct soul that set it apart from other cities. Ila, too, was captivated by the city's unique character, and Sukumar was content to watch it all go by.

For Yohan, Mumbai represented the pinnacle of his career. The speed, the freedom, and the feeling of everyone chasing something were intoxicating. Ila, on the other hand, was relieved that she could stay away from her home in Old Delhi. Her mother was behind her back to get married, as she was just a summer shy from turning 31, and being from an orthodox Muslim family, 31 was looked upon as an age where a suitable, 'pious', religious groom was out of the picture.

Sukumar, the only married man among the three, was still miffed that he had to stay away from his loving wife. Interestingly, he had met her during an assignment in Mumbai. But Sukumar's idea of Mumbai was different. Unlike Yohan, for whom South Bombay was the lifeline, and for Ila, who enjoyed the perks of the suburbs, Sukumar stayed far away in Panvel, which is considered 'Bhargaon' or out of the city by most Mumbaikars.

"Mohammed Rafi Saab was right," Sukumar didn't take too long to express his mind.

"Are you going to sing now, *anna*?" Ila knew Sukumar had multiple strengths, but the gift of music wasn't one of them. Yohan, on the other hand, had learned when to ignore Sukumar, so he kept to himself. Suddenly, to everyone's despair and the driver's shock, Sukumar started singing.

"Kahin building, kahin trams, kahin motors, kahin mills,
Milta hai yahaan sab kuch, ek milta nahi dil;
Insaan ka nahin kahin naam aur nishaan,
Zara hat ke, zara bach ke, yeh hai Bombay meri jaan."
(Translation:
Buildings, trams, motors, and mills.
You get everything here except a heart.
People don't have a name or identity here.
Keep away, keep safe; this is Bombay, my dear.)

Ila kept looking at the helpless driver, who had no choice but to bear this verbal assault at close quarters. "*Anna*, we get your point. I really want to read through all the information I received in the mail."

"Ila, you guys are Mumbai fanatics. You will never agree with me," Sukumar sighed. Yohan, a usually calm man, did not like the bashing that Sukumar had unleashed on Mumbai. More than anything else, he always loved to have the last word, and with Sukumar it was more of a banter. "If Rafi Sahib were alive, I would have sung back a response."

"*Arey*, boss will sing now," Sukumar was all charged up while Ila looked at her watch since she didn't have much hope from Yohan when it came to singing. But her generally quiet nature just prompted her to stay away from commenting.

"Yahaan dil hai, dilon mein pyaar bhi,
Yahaan insaan ka naam hai aur voh kamaane ka dariya bhi,
Arey socho mat, daro mat. Aayiye,
Yeh hai Mumbai, meri jaan."

(Translation:
This city has a heart filled with love.
Here, people have an identity earned by patience.
Think not, fear not. Just come.
This is Mumbai, my dear.)

Ila liked Yohan's wordplay, but she was absolutely right about his singing skills. To her and the driver's good fortune, their vehicle entered the premises of the Andheri East Police Station.

***

Yohan's voice boomed through the officer's compact cabin, his frustration palpable. "Isn't examining circumstantial evidence a fundamental aspect of any investigation, Kamble ji?" he roared, his eyes blazing with righteous anger. He looked around the room, taking in the sorry state of the local police's investigation. "The Mumbai police is world-renowned for its efficiency, yet your investigation is an affront to their capabilities," he thundered, his voice echoing off the walls.

Kamble cowered under the weight of Yohan's scathing words, sweat beading his forehead. He felt like a small child who was being chided by a stern teacher. His mind raced, searching for a way to defend his actions. "Sir, it appeared to be a straightforward case of a fire accident," he stammered.

Yohan stepped forward, his imposing figure looming over Kamble. "You have a duty to the people of this city, Kamble ji," he said, his voice low and dangerous. "And you have failed in that duty."

"The initial report clearly indicates the presence of an unknown individual, a gas leak, and so much more. How is this straightforward, Kamble sir?" Ila's voice dripped with aggression.

"You know what circumstantial evidence is, Kamble ji," Yohan snapped.

"Y-yes, sir," Kamble stuttered.

"It seems you don't, Kamble ji," Yohan said, his voice rising. "Why weren't footprints matched or surveillance footage reviewed? Why weren't guest entry lists checked or building residents questioned for suspicious activity? None of that appears in your report."

Yohan knew that any further conversation would yield little benefit. As frustration mounted for Ila and Yohan, Sukumar was outside making a series of phone calls, trying to gather as much information as possible.

Sukumar walked inside, rubbing his forehead as if he had something important to share. Yohan sensed his officer had something to say. He requested Siad Kamble and his team to wait outside as they needed the room to discuss the details of the case.

"I found some crucial information," Sukumar began, his tone serious.

Ila and Yohan asked Sukumar to enlighten them.

"I made a call to the CCTV firm, and they informed me that the visuals of the past two days were erased from the system," Sukumar said, his voice dripping with concern.

Ila and Yohan were shocked.

"What do you mean, erased?" Yohan asked, his brow furrowed.

"It seems someone tampered with the CCTV footage," Sukumar replied. "This is not a good sign. It means that someone is trying to cover up their tracks."

Yohan nodded in agreement. "This is a well-planned and executed murder," he said. "Everything – the fire, the wiring, the entry, the gas leak – seems to be part of a bigger plan."

"I think we need to go back to the crime scene and re-investigate everything," Ila added.

Yohan agreed, "Yes, we need to start from scratch."

"At least we have a starting point now," Sukumar added.

Yohan asked Ila if she knew where Adinarayan was staying since his house was burnt.

"He is staying in his company's guesthouse," Ila replied.

Yohan turned to Sukumar and said, "Coordinate with the local police and mark the place as a crime scene. Seal it off immediately. We need to get a team there right away to gather evidence."

Sukumar nodded, "Yes, sir. I'll get on it right away."

Yohan turned to Ila and asked, "Did you see the email your source sent about Mekhala's Delhi visits, especially the ones before she started working as a literary agent?"

Ila replied, "I just glanced through it."

Yohan asked, "Is there anything unusual?"

"It is difficult to draw firm conclusions," Ila said, pausing for a moment, "… I have also asked for Mekhala's bank statements to compare the data."

Sukumar asked, "Are you onto something?"

"I'm not sure yet, but there have been several deposits from accounts that don't seem to make sense," Ila said.

"What do you mean?" asked Sukumar.

Ila replied, “Mekhala has been receiving close to 80,000 Rupees from one account every month.” She pointed to the transaction data on her laptop.

Sukumar read out the name of the sender, “Trilok Publishers. Looks like a publishing house, but why does it look suspicious to you, considering she was an agent?”

Ila said, “On quick research, Trilok Publishers looks dubious. They have published just a few books, but Mekhala received money from them every month.”

Yohan interjected, “It looks like a cover for something, clearly. We need to dig deeper into this.”

Ila nodded in agreement, “I'll start tracing the source of these transactions and see if we can find any connections to the murder.”

Sukumar added, “Let's not rule out the possibility that the money trail and the murder could be connected.”

Yohan looked at them and said, “This could be the breakthrough we were looking for. Let's keep working on this and see where it leads us.”

As they were about to leave, Yohan suddenly stopped Ila and Sukumar, causing them to turn back with a look of confusion on their faces. “What's up, Yohan?” Ila asked, hoping it wasn't another twist in the case.

Yohan's expression was serious. “Ila, bring back your laptop,” he said firmly.

Ila quickly retrieved her laptop and brought it back to Yohan.

“Did you notice anything unusual in the data before Mekhala became an agent?” Yohan asked her, his eyes fixed on the screen.

Ila hesitated momentarily before admitting, “No, I didn't.”

Yohan leaned in and said, "Scroll up and see if you can find a pattern. Sukumar, you analyse it, too. We need to get to the bottom of this.'

Ila and Sukumar quickly got to work, poring over the data on Ila's laptop. As they went through the information, there was a sense of impatience in the room. Every passing second felt like an eternity. Yohan leaned against the wall and lit a cigarette. He knew they were onto something but needed more information to connect the dots.

After a few moments of silence, Sukumar spoke up, "This is strange. Look at these bank statements from before Mekhala became an agent."

"What is the strange part?" Yohan asked.

"She was receiving regular payments even before she became an agent," Ila added.

"But she did some corporate work, right? It could be from there," Yohan replied.

"These aren't from those companies," Sukumar added.

"He is right. I can see payments of 65,000 received every month from a company named Pucolite Industries," Ila said.

"Before that, Mekhala was receiving Rs 50,000 every month from another company called SBR Securities," Sukumar added.

Yohan processed the information and said they needed to dig up Mekhala's past in detail and get to the bottom of the issue.

"What does this mean?" Sukumar asked.

"It means that madam Mekhala Thampi has a past we are unaware of yet," Yohan walked towards the door as he spoke. "It also means it is time to meet my old friend, Mr. Adinarayan Mahendran."

***

Adinarayan sat in the lobby of his society premises in Chakala, his eyes fixed on the three investigating officers who were making their way towards him. He had already spoken to Sukumar over the phone and was eagerly anticipating their arrival. However, now that his house had been marked as a crime scene, even Adinarayan couldn't enter his own property without obtaining the necessary permissions.

Despite the tense situation, the journalist's attention was captured by one particular person—Yohan. Adinarayan couldn't help but notice Yohan's towering figure and his neatly shaped beard accentuating his chiselled jawline. Dressed in a white shirt and khaki pants, he looked like a dashing detective, complete with rectangular framed spectacles. To top it off, he was casually enjoying a Vada pav sandwich neatly wrapped in paper.

As the investigating team arrived, Adinarayan remained firmly seated, gesturing for them to take their places. "Hello, Sukumar," he greeted. His voice was calm but tinged with an air of formality.

Knowing fully that Adinarayan was not particularly fond of him, Yohan smiled wryly and nodded in acknowledgement.

"Hello, Mr. Adinarayan. I know this isn't the best time, but I must say, I am a huge fan of your reporting," Sukumar said, exchanging pleasantries and a few words to butter up the celebrity journalist. Yohan couldn't help but roll his eyes at this people-pleasing side of Sukumar, and waited to be introduced.

"This is Ila Qureshi, and meet our lead investigator... Mister…" Sukumar trailed off looking at Yohan expectantly.

"I know who he is," Adinarayan interjected, his words dripping with disdain, "Mr. Yohan Tytler, son of the cement tycoon Rajesh Tytler."

Despite the animosity between them, Yohan chose to remain professional. "Thank you for the introductions, Sukumar," he said with a polite nod. "I look forward to working with you, Mr. Adinarayan." Yohan chose to ignore the yesteryear rivalry between the journalist and his father.

The year was 2012, and Adinarayan was still a print journalist working for a reputed media firm. After months of tireless research, he uncovered a shocking truth about the cement industry that was transpiring right under the noses of the authorities. Adinarayan's story dominated the day's headlines, revealing that 12-15 top Indian cement companies, including the biggest ones, had formed a cartel to hike prices for the common man.

The news spread like wildfire, and the Competition Commission of India (CCI) launched an investigation into Adinarayan's claims. After the enquiry, most of Adi's assertions were proven true, and the select companies were fined over 6000 crores. Even Yohan's father, a cement tycoon himself, was forced to pay around 240 crores in 2012. Understandably, he was livid with Adinarayan and had vowed to exact revenge.

Rajesh Tytler, Yohan's father, rallied a group of powerful businessmen in his industry who happened to be significant advertisers in the newspaper where Adinarayan worked to withdraw their advertisements.

This put immense pressure on the media outlet and the journalist. Eventually, in a peace offering meeting, the newspaper editor agreed to consider Adinarayan as collateral damage and fired him from the job.

Following this incident, Adinarayan hit rock bottom. He had to knock on multiple doors for a job. Finally, as a desperate last resort, he joined the television channel News Now and eventually went on to become the celebrated crime reporter he was today. However, he never forgave Rajesh for what happened, and the turbulence he went through in life left a deep scar.

Sukumar started the conversation by asking Adinarayan, "When did you and Mekhala get married?"

" In 2016. About five years ago," Adi replied

Ila then turned to Adinarayan and asked, "Did you know the exact nature of Mekhala's job? Can you share particular details?"

Adinarayan felt a knot form in his stomach. His marriage with Mekhala had always been complicated, with both focused on their careers. He knew the officers wouldn't understand the dynamics of their relationship.

"To be honest, we never really talked about work," he said, his voice trailing off. "I knew she had started working just a year before our wedding, but I don't know much beyond that."

Yohan saw that the conversation was going exactly in the direction they wanted. He directed his first question at Adinarayan, "Did you know what Mekhala did before becoming an agent?"

Adinarayan acknowledged Yohan's question but chose to look at Sukumar while answering. "As far as I knew, she worked as a communications officer for some private company," he replied.

Ila acknowledged Adinarayan's answer and followed up with another question, "Did you have any knowledge of her financials or salaries?"

Adinarayan was suddenly outraged hearing this. His frustration was evident, as he finally turned to Yohan and asked, "What is going on here? Is this some big joke, or are you guys trying out a new torture method of the Tytler clan?" He rose from his seat, his voice rising with anger, "My wife is dead, and instead of investigating her murder, you guys are busy examining pointless details of her career ?"

Yohan replied, "Calm down, Adinarayan, we are just doing our job. Everyone is equal before the law, and being a celebrity journalist doesn't qualify you for receiving preferential treatment."

This further angered Adinarayan. He mumbled, "Bloody Tytlers!" and started to walk away, banging his chair on the way out. Sukumar went after him, trying to calm him down. "Please, Mr. Adinarayan, we need to ask these questions. It's standard procedure."

But Adinarayan was having none of it. He pushed Sukumar away and shouted, "Standard procedure, my foot! You guys are just trying to harass me because of the Tytlers. You know they have it in for me!"

Yohan, who was calm all this while, also stomped up and said, "Stop dragging my family and father's name into everything, Adinarayan."

Adi angrily responded with, "This investigation is bogus, and you guys are just pushing irrelevant details."

Sukumar stepped in, trying to diffuse the situation, "Adinarayan, we understand your frustration, but these things are connected to your wife's death. We need to look at all aspects of her life to uncover the truth."

Ila, who was observing the commotion all the while said, "Mr. Adinarayan, we have enough reason to believe that your wife's death was a well-planned murder, and these details are important to uncover the reason behind it." Her voice rose slightly as she continued, "Right now, Adinarayan, you are not cooperating, and that is stopping your wife from getting the justice she deserves."

Adinarayan's anger dissipated at Ila's words. He slowly walked back and took his seat, his mind lost in thought. After a moment of silence, he spoke up, "I understand what you are saying. Maybe there are some things I should tell you." He hesitated for a moment before continuing, "Our marriage was just a marriage of convenience. We were more like roommates than husband and wife." The journalist went on to explain the dynamics of his marriage.

Ila empathised with Adinarayan's situation and tried to make him feel more comfortable. "I can understand how difficult it must have been for you," she said softly.

Yohan, on the other hand, remained indifferent to Adinarayan's confession. He was still holding onto unresolved issues of the past and couldn't let them go. He stood there with a blank expression, his mind lost in thought.

Sukumar was taken aback by Adinarayan's revelation and struggled to find the right words to say. He couldn't comprehend how a married couple could be like that.

Ila leaned forward and asked, "Mr. Adinarayan, do you have any idea where these monthly credits to Mekhala's account were coming from because it was clearly not from her profession?"

Adinarayan had no clue about Ila's question. After a few moments of silence, Adinarayan suddenly remembered something, "Oh, wait, now that you mention it, Mekhala used to go to Delhi frequently."

Sukumar interjected and said, "We know that."

Adi said, "Yes, yes, but once, when I called one of her publisher's offices for some emergency, they said that she had not visited them at all." Adi further explained that he had then called Mekhala's phone, and someone else answered and said that Mekhala was busy in a meeting with an author and had to leave her phone outside.

Yohan asked, "Who was she meeting?"

Adi said, "I remember Mekhala mentioning a name to me when she returned. It was some Mustafa Shaikh or something."

Ila, impressed by Adi's memory, asked, "Why do you remember such a random name?"

Adi replied, "The fact that Mekhala had to leave her phone outside made me curious about who this person was. Besides, I'm a journalist and a good memory is a journalist's biggest asset."

"Who is Mustafa Shaikh? I've never heard that name," Sukumar quizzed.

As the team made notes, something was going on in Adinarayan's mind as he gave these details. He said, "I specifically remember Mekhala being very disturbed after this meeting. At least that's what I felt when she returned from Delhi."

Yohan asked, "When was this?"

"Last year in 2021, during the lockdown," Adi replied.

Yohan asked, "Why do you remember the date?"

Adi replied, "It was one of the first times I saw Mekhala that worried and concerned about something. I also remember it because it was the same time that a prominent Bollywood actor was found dead in his apartment, and Mekhala was subsequently upset on hearing that too since she really liked the actor."

Sukumar had also liked the same actor, but instead, he chose to focus on the other name that Adinarayan had dropped. "Who is this Mustafa Shaikh?" he asked yet again.

Chapter 5
ALL THAT GLITTERS ISN'T INNOCENT

Yohan and his team checked out of their hotel and headed towards the Government guesthouse allotted to them. The guesthouse was located in Bandra, a bustling suburb of Mumbai, and was not much to look at from the outside. However, the inside was equipped with large rooms that the team could use to discuss case facts, complete with numerous whiteboards and stationery supplies.

As soon as they arrived, Sukumar eagerly rushed to grab the best room, claiming it had the most comfortable bed. Ila and Yohan smiled at his child-like enthusiasm.

Once they were all settled in, Yohan called for a team meeting. They gathered in the living room, which was furnished with a couple of sofas and a coffee table.

"All right, let's get started," Yohan said, looking at his team. "Any new leads?"

Ila began, "I spoke to the publishers that Mekhala worked with. They have never heard of Mustafa Shaikh."

Yohan nodded, "That's not surprising. Adinarayan mentioned that she met him outside of work. I want you to dig deeper into Mustafa Shaikh's background. Find out who he is and how he is connected to Mekhala."

Ila jotted down the task in her notebook. "Do you think there's a strong angle there?" she asked.

Yohan replied firmly, "No aspect should be ignored. We have to look into every lead, no matter how small or insignificant it may seem."

Sukumar interjected, "But we still don't know how she got killed. We need to find some evidence or something to connect the dots."

Yohan nodded. "Yes, that's the ultimate goal. But we need to find a motive. We need to know why someone would want to kill her."

The team sat in silence for a moment, thinking about the possibilities.

Suddenly, Ila's phone rang. She excused herself from the room to take the call. When she came back, she looked grave.

"What's wrong?" Yohan asked.

Ila took a deep breath before answering, "The call was from one of my media sources in Delhi."

Yohan leaned forward in his seat, "What did he say?"

Ila looked at the team and took another deep breath, "Apparently, one of my source's friends, Mr. Preetam Gowda, was the journalist who unravelled the scam of the education business tycoon, Siju Sharatchandran. He was a Kerala-based businessman whose startup rose to a record valuation. He had taken more than 6500 crore loan from a public bank."

Sukumar's eyes widened in surprise. "That's a lot of money!"

Yohan suddenly asked, "Wait, is this the same businessman that Mekhala had a client writing a book about?"

Ila nodded slowly, "Yes, that's the same person."

Sukumar's face lit up, "Let me guess, Preetam Gowda was the whistleblower who exposed the scam?"

Ila nodded again, "That's what my source said. Apparently, he was the one who provided the crucial evidence that led to the exposure of Siju's hefty loan."

"So, we need to catch hold of Preetam Gowda to get more details," said Sukumar.

"That's the thing, Sukumar. He has been missing for more than 2 weeks," said Ila with a concerned look on her face.

Sukumar was stunned and spoke loudly, "Whattt?"

The air in the room grew thick with tension as the weight of the situation hit them. The officers exchanged glances, trying to process the gravity of the new information that had just been shared. The only sound that could be heard was the scratching of heads as they tried to make sense of it all. It was clear that this case had just taken a dark turn, and they had a lot of ground to cover.

"Yes, Sukumar. Mekhala was killed, and one of her clients is missing," Ila summed up.

"Guys, this case is getting serious. It's going to be a long ride," Yohan said. He then turned to Ila and said, "Make a list of all the clients and potentially controversial books Mekhala signed."

Sukumar intervened, "Should I pursue Mustafa Shaikh?"

"Go ahead," said Yohan. But he didn't stop there. "*Anna*, also check up on Pucolite Industries and SBR securities, the two firms that paid Mekhala regularly."

After rolling out the instructions, Yohan slowly walked towards the evidence board that had Mekhala's name with her information, details about Adinarayan, and a question mark next to Mustafa Shaikh. He took his favourite Mont Blanc pen from his pocket and added two more names: Preetam Gowda and Siju Sharatchandran.

"Mekhala is a woman with a mysterious past, and we need to unravel everything slowly," Yohan contemplated aloud.

Yohan's phone rang; it was Siad Kamble. Yohan hesitated for a moment and considered ignoring the call. But he wanted to give the inspector another chance. After all, Yohan was still a huge fan of the Mumbai Police Force.

"Yes, Mr. Kamble," Yohan answered, his eyes narrowing with suspicion.

Kamble spoke in a hushed tone, and Yohan's eyes widened as he heard each word. The officer's face had turned red with anxiousness.

"Thank you, Kamble ji. Can you come to our guest house immediately?" With that, Yohan ended the call.

The other officers in the room turned to Yohan and asked him to spill the beans.

"Guys, there is another twist in the case. And for that, we need Siad Kamble here," Yohan said, picking up the pen to add more details to the evidence board based on the newfound information he had received.

As Yohan wrote the names and drew connections on the board, the officers couldn't help but feel a sense of unease.

****

Anand Bhattacharya and his wife, Surabhi, had moved to Mumbai around three years ago. The couple seemed to have blended into the city, with Anand working in a leading private bank and Surabhi taking up a job as a teacher after her stint as a political strategist for a leading national party, the Indian Alliance Congress.

But there was more to Surabhi's exit from the political circle than met the eye. It was whispered in the corridors of power that Surabhi's departure was far from amicable. She had left the party due to several differences, and there were rumours that she had fed sensitive information to the media about the party's inner workings.

The consequences of her actions were not known, but it was speculated that she had made a few powerful enemies. The air around her had tensed, and people seemed wary of her. It was as if she had become a liability, and no one wanted to be associated with her.

Ila and Sukumar listened intently, their eyes fixed on Siad Kamble as he spoke. They had been waiting for a breakthrough in the case, and Kamble's words seemed to be leading them somewhere.

"You have to tell them who these people are, Kamble ji," Yohan intervened, breaking the tense silence.

"They are Mekhala and Adinarayan's neighbours," Kamble replied, a sly smile playing on his lips.

"How are they related to the case?" Ila asked, her curiosity piqued.

Kamble motioned to his Head Constable, who promptly brought him his laptop. Plugging in his pen drive, Kamble started playing the CCTV footage from different days. The footage was grainy and dark but clear enough to see the faces of the two women in question.

"While Adinarayan is right that he and his wife didn't know the neighbours, there are multiple footage of Mekhala meeting Surabhi in the hallway, and they would spend a lot of time talking to each other," Kamble said, pointing at the screen.

Sukumar's eyes widened in shock. "So you are insinuating that Surabhi and Mekhala were planning something?"

"It's possible, Sukumar ji," Kamble replied. "Considering the fact that she is a rebel and has been giving out information as an unnamed source, what if Mekhala was her connection to the media? Being a literary agent who also handled publicity for authors, Mekhala was well connected with the media."

Yohan was impressed with Kamble's attempt to redeem himself after a dismal initial investigation. He patted Kamble's back for being sharp, cross-checking the visuals, and establishing the connection. "Well done, Kamble ji. This is good work," Yohan said, his voice tinged with admiration.

Kamble beamed with pride, feeling recognised and appreciated for his efforts. It seemed like they were finally on the right track to solving the case.

Kamble took a step back, looking around the guesthouse. It was time for him to leave and give the investigators some space to discuss the case. He nodded to the group before exiting the room, leaving them to their discussion.

Ila's heightened emotions were evident as she said, "Yohan, seriously, where is this case heading? The suspects and twists so far are inversely proportional to any breakthroughs." She fidgeted with the pen in her hand, clearly feeling the pressure of the case.

Yohan remained unfazed, his cool demeanour starkly contrasting Ila's distress. "We're just getting started, Ila. Let's review what we have so far, and then I'll give you a bonus," he said, flashing a confident smile.

The word 'bonus' seemed to electrify Sukumar, and he chimed in eagerly, "Hey, Yohan, are you enrolling us in your father's company that gives out generous Diwali bonuses?" He winked at Yohan, clearly excited by Yohan's revelation of a cash bonus.

Yohan chuckled before getting serious, "Handling you is one thing. My father would have shot you by now. But let's get serious, *anna*. I don't know if it will be a bonus or a shock."

Ila ignored the banter and delved straight into summarising the key points of the case. "Mekhala's death, a meeting with the PM just before her demise, opposition pressure brings us in, a death that looks like an accident – is clearly a murder, the presence of an unknown individual, multiple unexplained credits to Mekhala's bank account, mysterious past before becoming a literary agent, disturbed after the Delhi visit, who is Mustafa Shaikh that enters the equation, the deceased neighbour, Surabhi, as a potential whistle-blower, and, adding to the complexity, Preetam Gowda, Mckhala's client, who exposed a loan scam perpetrated by businessman Siju, is now missing."

Sukumar's mouth was hanging open in shock as Ila finished her monologue. He couldn't help but wonder if she was some kind of AI robot programmed to retain and spew out information.

"Thanks, Ila. Your summary was on point," he said before Ila cut him off.

"Thanks, boss. Now, what is the bonus?" she asked eagerly.

Yohan smiled, knowing how much his team valued breakthroughs. "Well, after Siad called me and informed me of this case, I used my lunch break to dig up some information on Surabhi. I called a few sources from her former party to investigate," he explained.

Sukumar couldn't help but interject. "I must ask, how did the media not pick up on this angle?"

"Good point, Sukumar," Yohan acknowledged before continuing. "I wanted to know which leaders Surabhi worked closely with."

"I have a bad feeling that I know where this is going," Ila's brain was ticking as Yohan spoke. "You're a smart officer, Ila. I'm sure you're thinking the same thing I am," Yohan said with a confident smile on his face. "The man we're talking about is Kailash Mukherjee, the opposition leader," Yohan revealed, pushing the team into overwhelming shock as they realised just how many twists and turns this case was taking.

"What? The very guy who's on TV blaming the Prime Minister?" Sukumar exclaimed, his tone dramatic as the reality of the situation sunk in.

"Yes, guys," Yohan said with a serious tone. "Apparently, they had a big fallout, which led to Surabhi's exit." He paused for a moment and then added, "And that he never forgave her." The revelation just added another layer to the already complicated case.

As he had started talking about Kailash Mukherjee, Yohan had walked up to the evidence board and wrote down the name. He then turned to Ila and said, "Ila, take the night and make a list of Mekhala's clients."

"Yes, Boss," Ila replied promptly.

"Sukumar, look at Pucolite and the other one that made payments to Mekhala," Yohan instructed again, "Tomorrow evening, we have to discuss all of this and connect all the angles together." With that, Yohan walked towards the door, signalling the end of the meeting for the day.

"Why in the evening, boss? We can get this done by tomorrow morning," an enthusiastic Sukumar suggested.

"Well, I'm taking a quick trip to Delhi tonight to meet the Honourable Leader of the Opposition tomorrow morning," Yohan explained as he prepared to leave.

***

Yohan crossed the Patel Chowk metro and made his way to Rajaji Marg, a politically eminent area that housed the residences of several high-profile politicians. The streets were empty, as it was a quiet Sunday morning. The wide roads were adorned with dividers filled with greenery, and the footpaths were of the best quality one could find in the country. Every house in the area had heavy security, with guards stationed outside each gate and security cameras dotting the landscape. The houses mostly looked alike, with similar architecture and design, but each had its unique charm and grandeur. Despite the uniformity of the houses, the area had no high-rises, and the surrounding trees and greenery made it seem like an oasis in the midst of the bustling city. The area has been home to many stalwarts in Indian politics and governance, including former presidents Dr. APJ Abdul Kalam and Pranab Mukherjee. As Yohan approached the opposition leader's house, he couldn't help but feel a sense of awe and respect for the place that held such power and influence. He couldn't help but reminisce about his childhood visits to this area. His father, a shrewd businessman, had always been in close contact with politicians from across party lines, and they often visited the high-profile leaders who resided in the area. Now, as a seasoned officer of the law, Yohan found himself frequently coming back to the same streets in the line of duty.

Yohan finished the formalities at the gate and went inside Kailash Mukherjee's house. He was greeted by the leader's PA, Anthony Raju, a gentleman with extensive political experience. "Welcome, Mr. Yohan," Anthony said. "Mr. Mukherjee will be with you shortly."

"Thank you," Yohan replied.

Yohan took a seat and browsed through his phone, using the waiting time to read through the digital versions of the case file. As he did, he thought about his strategy for questioning the country's tallest opposition leader.

A few minutes later, Kailash Mukherjee entered the room. He was a tall, imposing figure in a white kurta pyjama and spectacles that were tied to a thread and hung on his chest. The man in his 60s looked younger than his age, thanks to his active lifestyle and healthy eating.

"Mr. Yohan," Mukherjee said, extending his hand. "It's a pleasure to meet you."

"The pleasure is all mine, Mr. Mukherjee," Yohan said.

"Tell me, Mr. Yohan," Mukherjee said, gesturing for Yohan to sit down. "To what do I owe the pleasure of meeting the lead investigator of the Mekhala Thampi murder case?"

"Actually, sir, I have come here to discuss the investigation," Yohan replied.

"Oh, wow," Mukherjee said with sarcasm. "Your Prime Minister wants his officer to brief me about the case. That's a first in our democracy."

"I'm not here on behalf of the Prime Minister," Yohan said. "I'm here on my behalf. We've received some information that led me to you." Yohan then went on to explain about Surabhi.

"What? Is Surabhi dead?" Kailash appeared surprised. "And why does that bear a connection to me?" The leader's tone suddenly appeared more serious.

Yohan continued, "We have sources that tell us that Surabhi's exit from the party was not amicable."

Kailash started clapping. "I accused the Prime Minister, and now he is using the CBI to frame me!" he said sarcastically.

Kailash was infuriated, but being a seasoned politician, he was well-trained to keep his calm.

"Even if Surabhi is dead, how is it connected to Mekhala's murder?" he asked nonchalantly.

Yohan tried to be as non-offensive as possible. "I am not at liberty to tell you that, sir."

Kailash's guard was up, and he replied, "Then I am not liable to give you any answers, too. I was courteous enough to meet you not because you are a CBI officer but because you are Rajesh's son."

The inclusion of his father's name didn't sit well with Yohan as he hated using his father's name for anything, especially because he had chosen this career and had garnered enough credibility to be recognised in his own right.

"Sir. I am not accusing you of anything. I know you want the truth in the Mekhala murder case, and I thought you would help me out," Yohan tried a diplomatic and non-questioning line.

Kailash sighed. "You must understand that I have difficulty trusting you, Yohan. After all, you are a representative of the government."

"No sir, you can trust me. I am not a government representative but an officer of the law," Yohan said. "I will not spare anyone, no matter how powerful the culprit is."

Kailash stood up. "Yohan, if you want to question me, get a warrant." He knew well enough what to speak and what not to speak. "I will tell you one thing, though. Do you know why we had to part ways with Surabhi?" Kailash asked.

"I heard that she was a whistleblower of sorts in the media," Yohan revealed little but enough to participate.

"Yeah, all that was later. But while working with us, she was phishing for a job with the ruling party. And guess who she was in touch with?" Kailash was throwing hints at Yohan.

"Who, sir?" Yohan asked.

"Prateek Sahni, the chief electoral strategist of your ruling party," Kailash answered. "And did you know that he was working with Mekhala on a book, but it was not released, and today, Mr. Sahni is no longer with the ruling party? Think, Yohan. See, whom all this is pointing towards."

Kailash walked back upstairs as Yohan stood in the leader's living room pondering and making note of the names and incidents the leader mentioned.

Chapter 6
INVESTIGATORS CAN'T BE CHOOSERS

"And we meet again, Mr. Investigator," a beautiful voice said from behind, tapping Yohan's shoulder. He turned around to see Shweta, the dashing journalist he had met during his previous Ashraf Zain murder investigation. Yohan immediately thought of all the fun Sukumar would have made had he seen Shweta.

Yohan and Shweta had planned to catch up for coffee at the Patna airport after the team solved the murder case and were on their way to Delhi. However, he never got the chance. Although it had only been less than two weeks since then, Yohan, who usually kept all his true emotions to himself, was extremely glad to see Shweta at the Mumbai airport but did not show it.

The Mekhala Thampi murder case was assuming multiple turns, creating several angles for them to investigate. But suddenly, for Yohan, the beautiful 5-feet 4-inches woman in her salwar and sling bag, ready to take on the world with a mic and questions using her journalistic abilities, was a pleasant sight. Yohan didn't even realise that he had frozen on seeing her, and the pause between her salutation and his response was getting longer.

"Hello? Yohan? Why are you lost, or are you checking me out?" Shweta asked with a smile.

"Hey, Shweta. What a pleasant surprise. I am just tired after a lot of travel back and forth," Yohan replied, trying to cover up his true feelings.

"We have a coffee pending. I believe you are not interested in that," Shweta said, hinting that she might have some feelings for Yohan, too. He was caught in a dilemma – he wanted to go out with her, but it was complicated with the ongoing murder investigation that now involved a prominent politician, and Shweta was a journalist – any information leak would make his life harder.

"Looks like you have a problem saying no. It's okay, I understand, Yohan," Shweta said as her excitement faded, turning to walk away with a heavy heart.

Yohan realised that Sukumar would have called him a fool for turning down the request, and it flashed in his head how, in such a beautiful situation involving a pretty woman, it was Sukumar's voice that came to his head. Without thinking further, Yohan called out, "Shweta… wait!"

Yohan blushed, seeing Shweta turn, "How about we have that coffee now?" He was decisive at his job but never confident in these situations. He would always wait for the other person to take the initiative, but with Shweta, there was always a thrill that had some danger due to their professions.

"Wow! An airport scene. Never pegged you for the filmy kinds, Mr. Investigator," Shweta made a jibe.

"I am not. This is very new to me," Yohan replied, feeling a little embarrassed.

"*Chalo* then. Let's get that coffee," Shweta insisted, grabbing his hand and leading him outside the domestic airport to a nearby coffee shop. The two seemed really into each other as they kept smiling and talking as they walked along. It was like the start of a new relationship, but neither party was aware of it. Shweta opened the door and guided Yohan inside.

"Before I get in, I must confess that I am a chai person," Shweta said, acting cute.

"I am neither a chai nor a coffee person. I am a fan of the company," Yohan replied, trying his hand at flirting.

Sensing that Yohan might have a tough time ordering, Shweta called for two '*Adrak wali chai*' with some onion fritters, a popular snack during the monsoon season in Mumbai. As they waited for their order, Shweta started a new conversation.

"So tell me, what case brings you to Mumbai, Mr. Investigator?" she asked with a curious smile.

Yohan was a little wary of the question and decided to lay down some ground rules. "Shweta, let's set two things straight right in the beginning, if that's okay with you," he said, trying to sound as polite as possible.

"Ooh, that sounds serious," Shweta quipped, looking taken aback.

"No, no. I was just thinking," Yohan replied. He continued with a playful tone, "First, please call me Yohan and not Mr. Investigator. That sounds so formal."

"Oh, come on. 'Investigator' has a hot ring to it, just like you," Shweta flirted back, her game on point. "And what's the second thing?"

"Let's not discuss cases, okay? You know the kind of pressure we investigators have," Yohan said, trying to sugarcoat his real reason for wanting to avoid work talk.

"Okay, that just makes me more curious, but I respect that," Shweta said maturely after Yohan declined to share the details of his work in Mumbai.

"So, what brings you here?" Yohan asked, attempting to steer the conversation in a new direction.

Being a journalist and someone with a penchant for last laughs, Shweta couldn't hold herself back from saying, "I thought we were not going to discuss work at all." She winked at Yohan, who laughed at her sense of humour.

"Oops. I should have been careful," Yohan replied, acknowledging her wit.

"Chill, ya. I am also here for work—a sensational case. The kind we crime reporters love," Shweta revealed. Yohan quickly realised that she was probably there to cover the same case that he and his team were investigating. In fact, Shweta seemed to have the same suspicion, given the extensive media coverage the case was garnering.

Suddenly, Shweta's attention was diverted to the television above Yohan's head. She noticed it because the screen had a photo of the very man sitting in front of her. Shweta's eyes widened, and she immediately directed Yohan's attention to the television.

Yohan was taken aback to see himself alongside the opposition leader, Kailash Mukherjee, on the television screen. Before he could comprehend the situation, Shweta rushed to the counter, grabbed the remote, and turned up the volume.

As the sound of Kailash's voice filled the cafe, Yohan listened intently to the accusations he was making against the Government and CBI's investigation. Shweta's eyes were fixed on the screen, her face mirroring the shock and surprise that Yohan was feeling.

"The Government is threatening me for raising suspicion on the Prime Minister in the Mekhala Thampi murder case," Kailash's voice boomed from the television. "They sent the CBI to investigate me instead. Is this how a responsible investigation should be held?"

Yohan felt a lump form in his throat as he heard the accusations. He knew that Kailash was a powerful and influential figure, and his words could cause a lot of damage.

Shweta, on the other hand, seemed more intrigued than scared.

"So, Yohan, I guess we are working on the same case again. Huh! Such a beautifully predictable plot twist," Shweta told him, her eyes still glued to the television screen.

*****

"Yohan, you should have informed me before meeting the Opposition Leader," CBI Director Jagat Verma's voice boomed through the speakerphone in his office in Delhi. Yohan immediately stood at attention. "Do you know what all I had to hear from the Home Minister? He trusted you with this case, Yohan, and I have immense pressure to pull you out of this," Verma continued, his frustration palpable.

"Sir, come on. You can't judge our investigation this early," Yohan tried to reason with Verma. We had clear proof to go and question Mr. Mukherjee. I will send you a detailed report. Please, show it to the Home Minister, and he will understand. In fact, he will tell us to go behind him."

"Fine, Yohan. Send it to me. I will show it to the Home Minister, but any similar action needs my approval henceforth," Verma calmed down a bit, but his anger persisted. Verma had always been like a rock for Yohan despite this outburst. Even though he was schooled, Yohan knew he had acted in haste.

"Of course, sir, I understand," Yohan replied, his voice low and respectful. "I will keep you in the loop from now on. And thank you for your support, sir. It means a lot to me and the team."

"Remember, I will protect you and the team as much as possible. But you must keep me in confidence. I will stand as a wall between you and any pressure as long as I am in the loop," Verma added. Yohan felt a rush of gratitude for his boss, who always had his back.

"Yohan, take care, son," Verma said, ending the call using a tone of assurance to ensure his officer's spirits weren't dampened.

The investigator kept the phone and turned towards his team members sitting in the conference room. The room was illuminated by a single dim bulb that hung from the ceiling, casting long shadows on the wooden table and chairs. The room was sparsely decorated with a few charts and posters on the wall and a bookshelf in one corner. Sukumar and Ila were sitting on opposite sides of the table, with their laptops and notebooks open in front of them.

"All okay, boss?" Sukumar asked Yohan, noticing his serious expression as he hung up the phone.

"Yeah, it's just bureaucracy, *anna*," Yohan replied. "Let's get back to work. So, what are your findings?"

Sukumar and Ila had toiled through the previous night and day to collect the information Yohan had requested.

Ila was eager to present her research. "So I went through Mekhala's clientele, which I must tell you is very extensive," she began, pulling out her diary to make a list. "The first lead we can pursue is a financial journalist, Mukut Apang, from Arunachal Pradesh. He unearthed a potential 10,000 crore financial scam that took place in India during the COVID era. He made a list of several loan apps, like Panda Cash, QwikRupee, RupeeInstant, etc., that have been disbursing easy loans to many Indians in dire need of cash. However, these apps resorted to threatening the users and extort more money from people, especially women."

"What was their *modus operandi*?" Yohan asked, intrigued.

"So, if people defaulted on payments, they would threaten the men by using the details they provided on the app, like photos and Aadhaar, and post on social media that they are '*chor*' or fraud. In the case of women, they would threaten to morph their pictures and post nude pictures on adult sites," Ila briefed the team, having done extensive research on the same.

"So, what's the connection, Ila?" a curious Sukumar asked.

"So Mukut apparently unearthed a connection between these apps and several businessmen running it. They were all funded by big investors, including foreign investments from the U.S., U.K., and China," Ila continued. "Mukut was approached by Mekhala, a proactive agent, to write about this and compile all his media stories into a book. She even told him that she could get him a deal from top publishers."

"So, did the book get published?" Yohan questioned. "Did you speak to Mukut Apang?"

"Yes, I did. He said he finished and submitted the draft to Mekhala, who was in the process of getting it published. But unfortunately, she passed away," Ila replied.

"Any specific reason you want us to pursue this?" Yohan asked.

"Yes, Yohan. So Mukut received multiple threats from a man named Himanta Barua, a powerful Assamese businessman running these apps. Mukut was even physically assaulted by Barua's henchmen," Ila briefed. "Mr. Himanta Barua didn't want this book released at any cost," she added.

"Definitely a lead we should pursue, Ila," Yohan appreciated his officer and wrote the names on his evidence board. "Any other leads, Ila?" he asked.

"So, Yohan, the second suspect, is also interesting," Ila began to brief her team with excitement in her voice. "Mekhala got in touch with a very senior employee of Brighter Tutorials, one of North India's biggest Engineering and Medical tutorials."

"What's with Mekhala and stories on scams in the education industry? First, Siju, and now this?" Yohan raised a valid point.

"That's a fair point, Yohan," Ila agreed. "But this is slightly different from Siju's case. Here, apparently, Mekhala's source, the former employee, revealed some shady parts of the business."

"Shady parts… former employee, it is all so vague. What is the name of the source?" Sukumar asked, his curiosity piqued.

"That's why it's interesting, Yohan. I have no idea who this source is nor what Mekhala was trying to expose," Ila added, her voice filled with intrigue.

"Now, I am wondering, why was Mekhala behind stories that had some or the other scam surrounding them? Why not normal stories?" Yohan chimed in, trying to connect the dots.

"Exactly, Yohan," Ila nodded. "And that is the larger point. Mekhala, as an agent, only focused on non-fiction and not fictional stories."

"If you don't know the source nor the story, how did you get this information?" Yohan asked, his curiosity mounting.

"This is what her publisher told me. This story was never brought to them, but Mekhala told them she had something big in store," Ila continued, her tone growing more intense.

"Who is this publisher?" Yohan asked, his eyes fixed on Ila.

"Sulochana Basu of Pangolin Publishers."

"Set up a meeting with her, Ila," Yohan requested, determined to get to the bottom of this case.

"Why her?" Ila questioned, confused as to why they needed to meet with the publisher when she wasn't a suspect.

"We need to understand what Mekhala was like as an agent. I think that's crucial to this case," Yohan clarified. "Also, Ila, these two suspects are based on two upcoming books she commissioned. Is there anything from the ones she has placed and has been published?"

"Yohan, that brings us to the next set of suspects," Ila said, her list ready. She had been hard at work, talking to Mekhala's publishers and writers and going through the books the illustrious agent had published.

"So, Yohan, have you heard of this app called AhaLife?" Ila asked.

Yeah, yeah, I have seen Sukumar watching videos on it when we are travelling. Very cringeworthy stuff. It's shut now, right?" Yohan replied, casting a strange glance at Sukumar.

"Hey, come on, boss. It was good entertainment," Sukumar defended himself.

"Yeah, sure, Sukumar," Ila said sarcastically. "But, Yohan, do you remember the controversy surrounding it?"

"Yes. Didn't they allow some political consulting firm to use their data during elections because a lot of people in rural India used or viewed these apps?" Yohan asked, recalling the details.

AhaLife was a content creation platform that had taken India by storm. People could make short videos, and they received likes and shares in return. The app monetised content creation, and securing a certain amount of viewership and engagement gave creators money. There was even a weekly leaderboard, and the top performers could win massive prizes such as Rs 1 crore, cars, laptops, and mobile phones. The app was initially popular in the cities but eventually spread its wings to rural India. A lot of content was created in Indian languages such as Hindi, Kannada, Oriya, Bengali, and others. Soon, AhaLife became an integral part of the lives of the common Indian.

However, in 2018, a debutant author, George Alfred, based in Bengaluru, released a book that made a massive revelation about the app's dangers. Alfred's book uncovered that AhaLife had exposed its data to a political consulting firm, InfoEdge Analytica. The consulting firm then helped several political parties influence people's voting behaviour, especially in the non-urban areas of India. They fed people with information that would influence their voting behaviour.

Many eminent people in the country, including actors, politicians, and sportspersons, used the app, and the eventual ban led to a lot of backlash from the public. The revelation of the app's involvement in politics had shaken the country's faith, and it had eventually shut down.

Yohan nodded, "Yes, I remember that controversy. But what does AhaLife have to do with Mekhala's case?"

"You mean apart from the fact that she commissioned the book?" Sukumar clarified, his sharp eyes fixed on Ila.

"Yeah…So the author, George Alfred, is missing," Ila said with a matter-of-fact tone that belied the gravity of the situation. But it was enough to increase the level of curiosity and suspicion in the minds of the other investigators.

"What? What do the local investigation reports say?" Yohan asked Ila, confident that she would have covered all bases.

"The Bengaluru police arrested one Mr. Saqib Sayed, one of the co-founders of the app," Ila confirmed, her voice low and serious. "But he was later released on account of lack of proof."

"Since when is he missing?" Sukumar asked, his mind racing to connect the dots.

"Since December 2019," Ila replied.

"More than 2 years. This is crazy, and still no signs of the author?"

"No, anna," Ila said.

Yohan was staring at the evidence board as his subordinates talked to each other. He was deep in thought, evaluating and processing the information. The evidence board was filled with pictures of the suspects, detailed notes of the investigation so far, and maps of the crime scenes.

"What are you thinking, Yohan?" Ila turned to her boss, waiting for his expert opinion.

Yohan took a deep breath and turned to face the others. "There's more to this case than meets the eye," he said, walking forward. "They could have hurt or kidnapped this author immediately after the release. But why wait for more than one year and then kidnap him?"

"That's a valid point," Ila agreed, her curiosity piqued. "Are you saying that the reason could be more than the book?"

"I think it is connected to his book, but there is something else here as well," Yohan said, his eyes fixated on the author's profile that he had googled on his phone. He took a moment off his phone and looked at Ila. "This is brilliant work, Ila. I can see the amount of effort and research you have put into this."

Ila, who never wore her emotions on her sleeve, was elated and felt recognised as she had spent hours and hours compiling all her information.

"I think the only thing that Ila didn't do is read George Alfred's book to gather more clues," Sukumar said, disguising a compliment with a jibe.

"Actually, anna..." Ila was about to tell Sukumar that she had already started reading the book, but she was interrupted by Sukumar. "No way. You are a machine, young woman," he said with a chuckle.

"Well, you could learn something, Sukumar. She is one up on you," Yohan taunted Sukumar, but it wasn't meant to be a serious jab at Sukumar's skills or abilities. Even Sukumar knew this, but the comment touched a raw nerve in him as he realised that Ila was ahead in the process, and that he may need to step up his game.

"That's because you still haven't asked me my findings yet, boss," Sukumar responded with a casual smile, but one loaded with his sense of purpose and conviction.

"Okay. That sounds interesting. Looks like my comment rubbed Anna the wrong way." Yohan figured that his words may have had more impact than he meant and tried to diffuse the slight tension brewing in Sukumar's mind. "Anna, before we get into that landmine you are sitting on, Ila, can you summarise your findings," Yohan requested.

Ila nodded and went on to brief her team. Her findings started with the proposed book by journalist Mukut Apang on financial crimes committed by several money-lending apps that misused personal information and the threats Mukut received from Himanta Barua, a powerful Assamese businessman who controlled most of these firms. Then Ila reiterated another book based on the revelations by an anonymous former employee of Brighter tutorials, but there wasn't much information available. The final one was a book on the controversy around Ahalife, a content creation app that exposed its user data to a political consulting firm, InfoEdge Analytica, and subsequently the missing author of the book, George Alfred.

"Ila, the Brighter Tutorials angle is very vague now. Find out more about its founders or anonymous employee from the publishing house you had mentioned. Talk to this Sulochana lady who is the publisher, " Yohan instructed Ila to cover all bases.

As Ila began to take notes on Yohan's request, Yohan turned to Sukumar. "Now, Anna, tell me about your findings," he said, addressing his longtime partner.

Sukumar took a deep breath, his eyes shining with excitement. “Boss, I think I might have stumbled onto something big.”

Yohan could see the thrill of the hunt, the rush of adrenaline that came with uncovering a major story on Sukumar's face.

“So you asked to check for information on both the companies that credited money to Mekhala's account,” Sukumar said, indicating that he had found something significant.

“Yes, anna. Go on,” Yohan urged, a little impatient and eager to hear what Sukumar had discovered.

“First, Trilok Publishers,” Sukumar began. “As we know, they have published just a few books, and now the most interesting thing: all the books are fiction. Strange, right?”

Yohan's face brightened with understanding, knowing very well what Sukumar was hinting at. “Of course, and we know Mekhala only dealt with non-fiction.”

“Good catch, anna. But how is this adding up?” Ila questioned, intrigued.

Sukumar acknowledged Ila's question. “Yeah, so with Trilok Publishers, it's just this strange connection, rather a disconnect. But things get much more interesting when we look at Pucolite.”

The atmosphere in the room was thick with suspense as Sukumar took a deep breath and began speaking. His colleagues, Yohan and Ila, watched him intently, their curiosity piqued. There was an undeniable tension in the air, as if they were all holding their breath, waiting for Sukumar to reveal something big.

“Pucolite is registered as a chemical company dealing in paints and adhesives,” Sukumar said, pausing for effect. “But when I dug deeper, I found something strange.”

Ila interrupted, "Stranger than the fact that a chemical company is paying a literary agent money monthly?"

Sukumar smiled wryly, "Let's say, even if we believe that angle, they had hired Mekhala as a communications consultant, so that can be justified." He was playing the devil's advocate, knowing well enough that he was withholding more significant information.

Yohan, eager for the reveal, said, "This better be good, Sukumar."

Sukumar continued, "Pucolite had filed annual reports as mandated by the Companies Act, but their turnover was less than 50 lakhs, which is much lower than what a chemical company would have, and by that means, Mekhala's salary isn't justified."

He paused for a moment, letting the significance of this sink in, before continuing, "They had several employees, and I am sure their salaries went into crores. I am still looking for all the employees lists, but using income tax data and cross-verifying it with the EPFO for PF, I came across the name of a former employee... one whose name will ring a bell in all our minds."

The room grew deathly silent as Sukumar spoke. It was as if the entire room was holding its breath, waiting for Sukumar to speak and shatter the fragile stillness that had descended upon them.

Yohan's impatience was palpable as he demanded, "Give us the name, already!"

Finally, Sukumar spoke those three words that would send shockwaves through the room, "Samar Singh Randhawa."

The weight of those words was immediately evident as Yohan and Ila exchanged a look of disbelief.

"The Bollywood actor?" Ila's voice quivered as she rose from her seat.

Sukumar confirmed her suspicion, "Yes, the very same man who was found dead in his apartment during Covid."

Yohan's jaw dropped in disbelief. The name Samar Singh Randhawa had been plastered all over the news when he was found dead in his apartment. The police had ruled it a suicide, but the media had a field day with theories of foul play. And now, here they were, investigating a possible connection between a Bollywood actor's death and the literary agent. The room was buzzing with excitement and tension as the implications of Sukumar's revelation sank in.

Chapter 7
SUSPECTS COME, SUSPECTS GO

Adinarayan sat alone in his hotel room, staring blankly at the wall. He couldn't bear the thought that his wife, Mekhala, had been murdered and the killer was still out there, roaming free. While she was alive, Adi never really indulged in their marriage of convenience. But her sudden loss made him realise the void that had been inflicted upon him. Adinarayan found himself caught in an unusual phase of life. He and Mekhala had carried the weight of past relationships they couldn't let go of. However, the one common thread that connected their love stories was the lack of approval from their respective parents. When they decided to tie the knot, they had agreed upon a partnership, a union, to avoid the alienation of society and simply have a lifelong roommate. Even their physical intimacy was transactional, driven by mutual benefits. Their unconventional marriage was a puzzle that no one could decipher if they ever found out about it.

Whenever they had the rare opportunity to meet, their drinking sessions became a voyage back into their past affairs, relishing the bittersweet memories. It was the most complex yet strangely simple marriage one could ever enter into. However, after Mekhala's tragic demise, Adinarayan found himself experiencing a newfound emotion toward her. He couldn't quite figure out if it was love, affection or something in between. One thing was certain, though: a righteous woman had been wronged, and as a result, he found himself enduring another heartbreak. Now, his sole solace in life would be seeking justice for his beloved partner. As he embarked on his quest for the truth, Adinarayan couldn't help but wonder if beneath the layers of their unconventional marriage there had always been a love waiting to be acknowledged, a love that had now been awakened by tragedy.

The CBI had been working on the case for days, but Adinarayan was not satisfied with their progress. He couldn't shake off the feeling that they were not doing enough.

"I can't just sit here and do nothing. I need to do something," Adinarayan muttered to himself, the frustration evident in his voice.

The media ruckus caused by the leader of the opposition, Kailash Mukherjee, had only added to Adinarayan's doubts. He believed that the investigation team led by Yohan Tytler was more interested in saving the Prime Minister's face than in finding Mekhala's killer. His preconceived notions about Yohan, primarily due to the bias that the CBI officer was the son of Rajesh Tytler, only added to his frustration.

"I can't just leave everything in the hands of bloody Rajesh Tytler's son," Adinarayan said, clenching his fists in anger.

He knew he had to take matters into his own hands. As an investigative journalist, Adinarayan had the contacts and resources to get to the bottom of things. He decided to reach out to Mekhala's close friends from her past, the ones she had introduced to him during the wedding. Since her parents were no more, Adinarayan hoped they could shed some light on Mekhala's life before they met.

The questions that the CBI team had asked about Mekhala's history had disturbed Adinarayan. He couldn't help but wonder why they were digging so deep into her past. As a crime reporter, he knew every detail could be crucial to solving the case. He had to find out more.

He stumbled upon the names of a few authors his wife had represented. He knew that Mekhala had commissioned most of their books through a publishing house called Pangolin Publishers. He decided to give them a call.

"Hello, Pangolin Publishers. How may I help you?" the voice on the other end of the line was a woman's.

"Hi, my name is Adinarayan. I'm calling about Mekhala. My wife was a literary agent, representing a few authors who had their books published through your publishing house. I was hoping to speak with someone who could shed some light on her work and maybe give me some insight into her life."

The woman on the phone paused for a moment, "I see. Well, I'm Nikita, PA to Sulochana Basu, the editor-in-chief at Pangolin Publishers."

"Hi, Nikita. Can you set up a meeting with Sulochana. I am sure she knows my wife," Adinarayan pushed.

"Sir, I knew Mekhala too. I am so sorry for your loss. I will set up a meeting and update you," the PA confirmed.

***

It was the year 2020 when the National and Regional media broke the news of the death of a very loved Bollywood lead actor. The actor was found dead in his house in Mumbai, sending shockwaves across the country. The news spread like wildfire, and people were reeling from the sudden loss of one of the industry's brightest stars.

The initial investigations on the case ruled it as a suicide, but there were a lot of things that weren't adding up. The media frenzy surrounding the case only grew, with different people speculating and theorising about what could have happened.

Ila, Yohan, and Sukumar sat in the spacious guest lobby of AhaLife, their eyes taking in the vibrant decor of the modern-day startup. The bright lighting and sleek white furniture were complemented by inspiring quotes and phrases from eminent personalities that adorned the walls. As they waited for the CEO, Anirban Chhetri, the trio couldn't help but admire the art that depicted freedom, expression, passion and similar life-like aspirations. The office was designed to attract and engage a young, energetic workforce, with facilities like an in-house creator studio, gym, indoor cricket, dance clubs and much more. Despite the grandeur of the office, their minds were elsewhere, thinking of the new lead and its connection to Mekhala's case.

"Do you guys think Samar Singh Randhawa's death has any connection to Mekhala's?" Ila turned to both Yohan and Sukumar.

"It's difficult to say anything with certainty, but the fact that a dubious organisation sent them money is suspicious," Yohan started. "Also, as per your findings, Samar was getting this money before his Bollywood career commenced."

"Yeah, so did Samar have a history like Mekhala that we don't know about?" Sukumar raised his eyebrow, his mind cooking up theories.

"Sukumar, get your number-crunching skills ready. Dig out the names of the other people who got paid by this company and track how many of them are dead or alive now," Yohan laid out the plan, determined to uncover the truth behind these mysterious deaths.

"Sure, boss. I can always give you another breakthrough. What say, Ila?" Sukumar joked, showing his competitive side.

Ila chuckled, knowing Sukumar well enough by now to not take his taunts very seriously. "Once is luck; twice is more believable," she replied.

Ila's gentle jibe away from her usual introverted nature put a smile on Yohan's face. He was happy to see how comfortable she had gotten with the team after her more conservative approach in the previous one. His smile showed a leader's satisfaction seeing his team mature.

As they discussed further, the receptionist interrupted them, "Excuse me, sir. Mr. Chettri is ready to meet you in his cabin."

The trio got up from their seats while Sukumar acknowledged the receptionist and walked towards the CEO's cabin.

Anirban Chettri's room was unlike any other office in the city. As soon as they stepped inside, the trio was struck by the opulence of the space. It was the kind of room that would make any CEO put it on their wish list. The first thing that caught their eye was the large glass window that overlooked Marine Drive. The company had paid a hefty sum to secure this privilege of a sea-facing office in a city where residential and commercial rentals hiked up at the drop of a hat. The view was breathtaking, with the waves crashing against the shore in a rhythmic dance.

The CEO's office was nothing less than a presidential suite in an elite hotel. The marble flooring shone in the afternoon sun, and the large white table made of imported wood was a testament to the luxury of the space. The chairs were no less impressive, with backrests that could soothe anyone's back. Walking towards the CEO's desk, they noticed the lavish sofas and the mini golf stand. A billiards table stood in one corner, beckoning anyone who wanted to take a quick break from work. It was the kind of space that even films with high budgets never portrayed while showing a CEO's office.

"Welcome, Mr. Yohan. It's a pleasure to host you and your team at AhaLife," said Anirban Chettri with a warm smile and a welcoming personality.

"Thank you, Mr. Chettri. You have a very beautiful office," Yohan exchanged pleasantries.

"Very kind words. Can I get you something to drink? Tea, coffee or if you would prefer something healthy like bitter gourd juice?" Anirban played the host well.

Ila felt that Anirban was trying too hard to impress them, and she wanted to get straight to the point. Meanwhile, Sukumar was crunching numbers in his head, trying to estimate the office setup cost.

"Mr. Anirban, if you don't mind, can we start by asking a few questions? Unfortunately, we are on a strict deadline here," Yohan spoke what was on Ila's mind.

"Of course. You are officers of the law, and I respect your time. I have just called my lawyer, Mr. Vikas here. It's company policy to have legal counsel while talking to any state machinery," Anirban explained, showing his professionalism and cautiousness. Neatly dressed in his black t-shirt and grey cargos, Anirban exuded a simplistic yet charming persona that added to his personality. He had a medium height with a well-sculpted body, giving the impression that he worked out regularly. His words always came across as politically correct, and there was a certain sense of humility in his interactions that even Ila appreciated.

"So, Mr. Anirban, we are here to ask you a few questions regarding the death of Mekhala Thampi," Ila began, taking charge of the proceedings.

"Whoa. Death? I don't know Ms. Thampi apart from what I've heard in the news," Anirban quickly clarified, his expression displaying genuine surprise.

"But you might know one, Mr. George Alfred," Sukumar chimed in, interjecting with an important point.

"I won't lie. Of course, I know him. We suffered a lot due to the misinformation he spread. We have filed a case against him. Vikas can give you the details," Anirban responded, gesturing toward his lawyer, who nodded in agreement.

"The thing is, Mr. Chettri, George is missing," Yohan added. "Considering your history with him, we have to believe that you and your office may have something to do with his disappearance."

Anirban's face turned serious, but he kept his cool as he considered Yohan's accusation. He sat back in his chair and sighed before responding, "I understand your concerns, but I assure you that we have no involvement in George's disappearance. Our legal battle with him is strictly within the boundaries of the law. I suggest you look into other leads."

"The thing is, Anirban, we believe that it has nothing to do with George's first book," Ila confirmed, her voice carrying a sense of conviction.

"Thank you, madam," Anirban replied, his restlessness apparent, but he maintained his composure and extended his gratitude.

"Yes. George went missing a year later, and we have information that he was planning a sequel to the book. Before its release, he was taken," Yohan revealed, sharing insights gathered from George's publisher during their research.

"That's a false accusation, Mr. Yohan. My client is cooperating, but it doesn't mean you can hurl anything at him or his company," Vikas, the lawyer, interjected, his voice laced with a hint of defensiveness.

"I understand, Mr. Vikas, but George received intimidating calls from your office, and sources close to him have confirmed that," Yohan persisted, refusing to back down.

"Don't believe in whataboutery by individuals who want to paint us as villains," Anirban countered, skilfully twisting the accusation and deflecting the blame.

"Okay, let's move on," Yohan said, realising that challenging Anirban with a lawyer present might not yield satisfactory responses. "Your app has been banned, but why are you still operating?"

"We are actively speaking to the government. Our advocacy team is tirelessly working to get the ban reversed. Additionally, we can't simply let go of all our employees because they believed in us and joined our mission for a freer and more expressive India," Anirban skilfully played the narrative game, emphasising the importance of their employees.

The atmosphere in the room grew tense as the conversation delved deeper into the intricacies surrounding AhaLife and its alleged connections to both Mekhala's death and George's disappearance.

"We had to lay off some people as part of our cost-cutting, but we are fighting the string of misinformation that has hit our business. Why would we kidnap Mr. Alfred when we are moving against him legally?" Anirban confidently presented his pre-meditated answers, clarifying any doubts surrounding his company.

"Well, you could have saved costs and jobs by just letting go of this fancy palace," Sukumar muttered to himself as he took notes, loud enough for Yohan to hear. Yohan couldn't help but roll his eyes at his colleague's remark, knowing it wouldn't contribute much to the conversation.

"So, Anirban, you work with a lot of celebrities, too, right? I mean, many of them have used your platform. Any interaction with Samar Singh Randhawa?" Yohan smoothly shifted the focus, introducing another angle into the discussion.

"Samar? Um, no. He never used our platform," Anirban clarified, a hint of confusion in his voice. "But why do you ask?" The CEO seemed genuinely perplexed by the sudden mention of the actor.

"Nothing, just felt he would have been a good ambassador for you guys," Yohan tried to downplay the significance of his question, concealing his true intentions for now.

Sukumar, who had remained unusually quiet for a long time, diligently taking notes and observing the conversation, finally cleared his throat, signalling his readiness to ask another question.

"Mr. Anirban, why is it that people who come in touch with you or your company often go missing?" Sukumar shot a direct question, cutting through the veiled exchanges.

"Mr. Sukumar, as I reiterated, we have nothing to do with George Alfred's disappearance," Anirban's tone carried a hint of irritation, his patience waning.

"No, no, sir. I was referring to Saloni Dutta," Sukumar dropped a name that hadn't been mentioned in the case so far, intentionally bringing a new element to the conversation. The CBI sub-inspector, known for his impactful data analysis and revelations, had chosen his moment carefully.

"I'm sorry, who?" Anirban inquired, genuinely unaware. However, before he could receive an answer, Vikas swiftly caught his hand and said, "Sir, she was in my team. She left some time back." The lawyer's intervention provided Anirban with the necessary information.

"Oh, sorry. I sometimes forget the names of employees who have left," Anirban responded, his tone becoming more composed.

"Surprising you forgot her, considering she had filed a harassment case against you. She left then and went missing a few days later," Sukumar stated, his research coming to fruition. Yohan and Ila noticed a thin layer of sweat forming on Anirban's forehead, a subtle sign of discomfort. The revelation of Saloni Dutta's involvement had struck a nerve.

"Oh, yes! That lady. Honestly, my legal team takes care of all these false allegations," Anirban shielded his irritation as much as possible, trying to maintain his composure under the scrutiny.

"But you were in a POSH meeting with her and an external consultant," Sukumar interjected, leveraging the information he had acquired regarding the 'Prevention of Sexual Harassment' meeting that had taken place in AhaLife's office.

"Oh, yeah. Her. I remember now. Sorry for my bad memory," Anirban attempted to salvage the situation with a touch of charm, hoping to deflect any suspicion.

"Aha... Life... Happens!" Sukumar finally unleashed the witty line he had been holding onto for far too long, silently patting himself on the back for the clever retort.

"What does that have to do with this case, officers?" Anirban's attorney, Vikas, interjected, trying to bring some order to the conversation.

"Nothing. It merely illustrates that your client and his company have a history of similar instances where opposing voices go missing," Yohan snapped.

"I think this discussion is over. Please, obtain an official warrant if you have any evidence, which I am certain you don't have since my client is innocent," Vikas declared, sensing that it was the opportune moment to put a halt to the proceedings and relieve his employer from further headaches

***

"Hello, Sulochana. Thank you for taking the time to meet me," Adinarayan greeted as he settled into the office of Pangolin Publisher's editor-in-chief. The office, located in Gurgaon within the Delhi-NCR region, provided a quiet and professional setting for their conversation.

"Hello, Mr. Adinarayan. It's my pleasure to help you in any way I can," Sulochana replied warmly, her voice carrying a tinge of sadness. "Mekhala was such an important part of our industry. She always brought stories that must be told to India."

Sulochana's words evoked a wave of memories for Adinarayan, reminding him of his wife's passion for her work as a literary agent. With a deep breath, he began to explain his objective. "Sulochana, I am trying to find the truth behind my wife's murder. For that, I need to know the authors she worked with. Can you provide any insights or anything unusual that you came across?"

Sulochana opened her laptop, revealing a Google sheet with a meticulously organised tracker of agents and their respective authors. The sheet contained submission dates, progress updates, and other relevant details. As she scrolled through the document, she began briefing Adinarayan about each of Mekhala's projects.

"This is the only unusual thing that struck me," Sulochana pointed to a particular entry in the sheet. It indicated George Alfred's name, followed by the words "ON HOLD" and a reference to a book associated with AhaLife.

Adinarayan's curiosity was instantly piqued. "When did you last meet Alfred?" he inquired.

"It was maybe a month or so before he went missing, along with Mekhala," Sulochana replied promptly, her voice tinged with concern.

Adinarayan sensed an angle worth exploring. "Why did they come to meet you?" he pressed further, his instincts as a journalist kicking in.

Sulochana took a deep breath, her brows furrowing as she recalled the encounter. "So, AhaLife was a book that garnered moderate success economically but created a huge media hype," she explained. "Alfred mentioned that he had additional information for a potential sequel, something new that had come to his attention."

"What kind of new information? Was it related to the shocking InfoEdge Analytica connection?" Adinarayan's mind was racing to connect the dots. He remembered seeing the book on his wife's bookshelf and had read it, finding it intriguing and thought-provoking.

Suddenly, Sulochana's eyes wandered upward, a subtle indication that she was deep in thought, trying to recall a specific detail. As her gaze returned to Adinarayan, she spoke with a newfound sense of recollection. "There was something unusual, Mr. Adinarayan," she began, her voice filled with intrigue.

"What was it?" Adinarayan leaned in, eager to uncover any potential lead that could shed light on the enigma surrounding Mekhala's disappearance.

"I vividly remember Alfred preparing to share something more with me, but Mekhala abruptly stopped him," Sulochana revealed, her words hanging in the air.

"Did you ask her why?" he inquired

"At that moment, I thought it was a matter between an agent and her author, so I respected their privacy and didn't press for an explanation."

Adinarayan's mind raced with a myriad of questions, but he realised that Sulochana might not have the answers he sought. Composing himself, he redirected the conversation toward a more tangible lead. "Sulochana, you mentioned that Alfred had a sequel in the works, right?"

"Yes,"

"Then there must be someone within AhaLife who had been providing information to Alfred," Adinarayan hypothesised, his tone tinged with determination. "Did Alfred ever mention anything about such an individual?"

Sulochana nodded emphatically. "Yes, there is. I recall him mentioning it once, though he didn't go into much detail."

"Great. Now, I need to find that person," Adinarayan declared, his mind racing with possibilities. The missing author, the book on AhaLife, and the potential secrets hidden within its pages were beginning to align, pointing to a web of intrigue that Mekhala had unwittingly found herself entangled in.

Chapter 8
A CONNECTION ON TIME SAVES NINE

"It has been a week since the CBI intervened in the Mekhala Thampi murder case," the journalist in the blue suit and red tie exclaimed. "However, apart from trying to scare voices in the opposition, we see no breakthrough in this sensational murder case. Is the CBI sleeping? Is Yohan Tytler and his team capable of giving us answers? Today, we will be discussing the top failures that the CBI has encountered in the recent past in our special segment 'CBI versus the Truth'." He lashed out as if he had some sort of personal animosity with the organisation.

Yohan and his team had skilfully kept their investigation away from the prying eyes of the media, save for the interrogation of Kailash Mukherjee. They knew the importance of preserving the integrity of their work and avoiding unnecessary distractions.

Visibly angered by the one-sided reportage, Sukumar lashed out in front of the team. "When we don't provide them with any information, they simply create their own narratives to fill the void," he exclaimed, his frustration evident.

Ila chimed in, her voice filled with exasperation. "The irresponsible and unaccountable media has become the biggest curse we are facing as a nation," she lamented. "It feels like we have to fight against these unimportant people while also working tirelessly to seek justice."

Understanding the impact of media scrutiny, Yohan tried to raise his team's morale. "Ila, as you mentioned, 'unimportant' is the keyword here. We have dealt with such situations in the past, and we shall overcome this as well," he reassured, his voice firm. He then turned his attention to Sukumar. "Sukumar, did you retrieve the list of employees who were formerly employed by Pucolite, Trilok Publishers and SBR Securities?"

Sukumar nodded, reaching into his folder to retrieve the list. "Yes, I have it right here," he confirmed, passing it to Yohan for further examination. Yohan accepted the list, his eyes scanning the names as he muttered them aloud for everyone's benefit. "Neha Sen, Sudipto Sarkar, Prakash Baruah, Ashish Chandy, Mira Gowda, Zulekha Ansari, Pritam Shah, Louis Wangmo..."

Ila's voice cut through the air, filled with a mix of surprise and recognition. "Wait, wait. Did you say Zulekha Ansari?" she interjected.

Yohan turned his attention to Ila, his curiosity piqued. "Yes, Ila. Why? Does that name ring a bell?" he inquired, eager to uncover potential leads. "Sukumar, do we have any information on which organisation was paying Zulekha?"

Sukumar swiftly checked his files, searching for the relevant details. "One moment," he replied, flipping through the pages. "It looks like Zulekha was associated with Trilok Publishers."

Yohan's eyes widened with intrigue. "Wait! Is she an author?" he questioned.

Sukumar shook his head. "No, she doesn't seem to be an author."

Meanwhile, Ila feverishly searched through her notes, desperately trying to recall where she had come across the name. She frantically flipped through the pages, hoping to stumble upon the missing puzzle piece that could shed light on Zulekha Ansari's significance in their investigation.

"Yes! Got it! But there's a problem; it seems to be a good one in a weird way, though," Ila exclaimed, her voice filled with excitement. Her associates eagerly awaited a clear answer, their curiosity mounting.

"Since when did Sukumar's disease of talking in code and building suspense infect you, Ila?" Yohan joked, attempting to break the tension that hung in the air.

"Sorry, guys. So, Zulekha was a content creator on AhaLife, one of their top performers," Ila revealed, finally getting to the point. "I was preparing a list of their top performers when I stumbled upon her."

"Interesting. But what is the 'good' problem, Ila?" Sukumar inquired.

"Her connection is not just with AhaLife," Ila added, fuelling the intrigue surrounding Zulekha Ansari.

"Then?" Sukumar probed further.

"She was also an employee of Brighter Tutorials," Ila disclosed, revealing another direct connection to one of the books Mekhala had commissioned.

"What did she do there?" Sukumar continued to dig deeper.

"She worked as a student counsellor," Ila replied, presenting her findings in the form of Zulekha's biodata sourced from LinkedIn. After glancing at it briefly, Sukumar excused himself to make an important phone call.

"Wait, Ila. So there was an anonymous employee giving information about Brighter Tutorials," Yohan interjected, connecting the dots, "And Zulekha received monthly credits from Trilok Publishers without publishing a single book. It's all adding up, Ila."

"What's your angle, Yohan?" she asked.

"Simple. It's possible that Zulekha maybe the employee, and I am certain that she was receiving these credits even before she left Brighter Tutorials," Yohan confidently laid out his assumptions.

Ila quickly cross-verified the information. "Yeah, you're right, Yohan. But why?"

"Clearly, Zulekha was planted there by someone. That job was just a cover," Yohan pieced together the puzzles.

"Are you hinting at corporate espionage?" Ila questioned.

"It's possible. You can look into it. Who would be Brighter's competitor?" Yohan advised.

"Clearly, Siju Ramachandran as well," Ila hypothesised, suggesting another potential connection.

"Dig deeper, Ila," Yohan instructed. "By the way, what was her AhaLife channel about?"

"Oh, she was a Yoga enthusiast. She used her channel to share yoga-related content," Ila quickly divulged.

"Okay. Interesting. And where was she based?" Yohan persisted, eager to uncover more details.

"Delhi."

"In that case, you know what to cross-verify," Yohan instructed Ila, signalling her to check if there had been any connection between Mekhala and Zulekha during their time in Delhi.

Meanwhile, Sukumar walked into the room, his face displaying a hint of displeasure. The atmosphere tensed as everyone turned their attention to him.

"Okay, break it, Sukumar," Yohan urged, knowing that Sukumar had news to deliver.

"Bad news, people," Sukumar began, his tone reflecting the gravity of the situation.

Yohan and Ila leaned in, their anticipation growing. However, Yohan couldn't resist interjecting before Sukumar could reveal the details, "Let me make a calculated guess. She is no longer alive."

Sukumar's face lifted in surprise, "Exactly. How did you guess that?"

"It seemed like the likely ending for Zulekha. I'm guessing she was going to author the book on Brighter Tutorials," Yohan clarified, his deductive reasoning at work. "Now, we need to establish the connection between her and Mekhala and uncover what they were planning."

With each new revelation, the case expanded, taking on new dimensions and demanding the full attention of the investigative trio. As the threads unravelled, their pursuit of the truth became more intricate and complex.

*****

"Sukumar, just show Verma sir the chronology of the deaths so far," Yohan instructed *anna*; their team was gathered at the CBI headquarters in Delhi. They had come to the capital city to gather more information about Zulekha, her life, and her mysterious disappearance leading to her death.

"Hold on a second, Sukumar. Let me connect this video call," Jagat Verma, the CBI Director, interjected. He quickly connected the call and turned his laptop towards the team. The Home Minister, Mr. Arvind Shankar, appeared on the screen, joining from his office at the North Block, Central Secretariat.

"Thank you, Mr. Verma. How are you guys?" Minister Shankar greeted his officers.

"Sir, we are fine. We were just about to brief Verma sir on the case's progress so far," Yohan responded, surprised by the unexpected presence of the Home Minister. Despite the sudden turn of events, the team chose to remain focused on the task at hand.

"Of course, yes. I also want to see where things stand," Mr. Shankar replied, displaying a keen interest in the investigation.

Yohan turned to Sukumar, who was prepared to provide the necessary explanation. Sukumar began by outlining the methods they had employed and the connections they had established, leading them to their current findings.

"The thing is, we believe these murders are connected to each other. First, Zulekha in May 2019, then actor Samar Singh Randhawa in September 2020, and most recently, Mekhala Thampi in February 2022," Sukumar briefed the Home Minister.

"Hmm. Yohan, can you tell me how you people connected these murders?" the Home Minister inquired.

Yohan opened his presentation notes, displaying the information for the Home Minister. He explained the trail of credits from different organisations and demonstrated the connections they had uncovered.

"Okay. And what about Kailash Mukherjee?" the Minister inquired.

"So far, we only have a connection between Kailash and Mekhala," Yohan replied, discussing the angle of Mekhala's relationship with her neighbour, a former employee of Kailash's party.

"Good going, team. I will drop off now. But make sure you come to a resolution soon. The Prime Minister is closely following this case," Minister Shankar stated. He concluded with a final piece of advice, "Also, if you stumble upon anything unusual or controversial, get in touch with me directly before taking any action."

"Sure, sir," Yohan acknowledged.

"Just get in touch with Samuel, and he will set up a meeting," Minister Shankar referred to his OSD (Officer on Special Duty) Samuel Narzary, a former Harvard and JNU graduate who hailed from Manipur. The Minister immediately ended the call, leaving a sense of intrigue in the room.

"Yohan, do you sense any pattern here, or are these random murders?" Jagat Verma questioned.

"Sir, that's the trickiest part of this case. Each murder has a different *modus operandi*," Yohan replied, pulling out a file containing detailed descriptions of each incident. "For instance, Zulekha went missing in April 2019 and was later found dead in a hotel room in Delhi. She was poisoned, and the hotel staff had to break open her door after she didn't respond to check-out calls."

"And, just so you know, Housekeeping didn't ring the bell because her door had a 'Do Not Disturb' sign on it," Sukumar added.

"Any suspects?" Verma inquired.

"No, sir. The Delhi police questioned the hotel staff, but nothing concrete came up," Ila informed.

"We're all aware of Samar Singh's death. The media had a field day with it, and it remains a mystery," Yohan explained.

"Do you believe the suicide theory?" Verma asked.

"We need to explore that angle further and determine if the strangulation marks were truly from a suicide attempt or if external pressure was involved," Yohan responded promptly.

"And Mekhala's death was due to a fire accident," Verma confirmed. "Did these three individuals ever meet?"

"We don't have any information yet. But our best guess is that Zulekha was the one who was about to write a book exposing malpractices in the education industry, specifically involving Brighter Tutorials," Ila added.

"Why are we not pursuing the angle of Samar's death?" Verma questioned.

"Well, sir, we have learned from you to do everything right but stay out of the media's eye," Yohan indicated the circus that would ensue if they reopened the investigation into Samar's death without solid leads, with a twinge of sarcasm.

"You're learning well," Verma chuckled. "So, what's the next plan of action?"

"Now, Zulekha discovered something about Brighter Tutorials. We need to uncover what that was," Yohan stated. "And not only that, another journalist named Preetam Gowda, who was about to expose another education sector scam involving Siju Ramachandran, is also missing." Yohan informed them about the additional angle they were exploring.

Sukumar interjected, his voice filled with concern. "Another crucial aspect we must consider is the disappearance of Mekhala's authors."

Yohan scratched his eyebrow, realising the gravity of Sukumar's observation. "You're right, Sukumar. It's highly suspicious that the authors associated with Mekhala have also vanished. There could be a deeper connection between them and the motive behind these disappearances."

****

Yohan and his team entered the imposing five-story building of Brighter Tutorials, located in the upscale Safdarjung Enclave of South Delhi. The bustling market of Safdarjung Development Authority stood nearby, adding to the vibrant atmosphere of the area. The team made their way through the entrance and headed straight to the office of the company's Chief Executive Officer, Bill Charles.

As they reached Bill's office, they found him engrossed in some documents. He looked up, surprised to see Yohan and his team standing in his doorway.

Yohan flashed his CBI ID card.

"Good afternoon, Mr. Charles. Apologies for the unannounced visit, but we need to speak with you regarding a serious matter," Yohan introduced himself, extending his hand.

Bill, a middle-aged Goan Christian with a calm demeanour, shook Yohan's hand and motioned for the team to enter. "Of course, Inspector Yohan. Please have a seat."

The atmosphere Inside Bill's office was more subdued than Anirban Chettri's extravagant office at AhaLife. Yohan, Ila, and Sukumar took their seats, preparing to question the executive.

"How can I help you?" Bill asked, his tone polite but slightly guarded.

"We are here to inquire about one of your former employees, Zulekha Ansari," Ila stated directly, cutting to the chase.

Bill's face showed immediate recognition, "Ah, yes. Zulekha. She was found dead under mysterious circumstances."

"It is precisely that mystery we are trying to unravel, Mr. Bill. We would like to know more about Zulekha as an employee," Sukumar pressed.

"To be honest, I didn't work directly with her. She was part of the Marketing team," Bill responded promptly.

"Did you ever hear of any complaints or issues related to her work?" Ila inquired.

"Why don't I put you in touch with her manager?" Bill suggested, realising that he might not have the specific information they sought. He called his security personnel to bring in the Head of Marketing.

As the team continued discussing with Bill, a tall, well-built man in his early forties entered the room. It was Pranjal Sahni, the Marketing Head of Brighter Tutorials.

"Meet Pranjal Sahni, our Marketing Head," Bill introduced, gesturing towards Pranjal. "Pranjal, why don't you take our guests, these officers, to a meeting room and cooperate with them."

Pranjal nodded in acknowledgment and directed Yohan, Ila, and Sukumar to a nearby meeting room.

"Pranjal, let's cut to the chase. We need to know what you thought of Zulekha as an employee," Yohan got straight to the point.

Pranjal was slightly taken aback by the immediate interrogation. "She was above average at her work, at best," he responded.

"Why do you say that?" Ila inquired, curious to delve deeper into Pranjal's opinion.

"She did the bare minimum that was asked of her. Most of the time, she would spend her time on chai and cigarette breaks," Pranjal candidly expressed his lack of high regard for his former teammate. "I apologise if it sounds harsh, but I am being honest about her performance as an employee, distinct from her as a person."

Ila appreciated Pranjal's no-nonsense approach, especially because she expected more spins and faffs from a marketer.

"Did she get into any sort of trouble here?" Ila followed up.

"Oh, you don't know? We were actually planning to fire her," Pranjal revealed without hesitation.

"But she was still an employee when she was found dead," Sukumar interjected.

"Yes, that's because she absconded one fine day after we started conducting an inquiry," Pranjal clarified.

"So, you didn't fire her?" Yohan questioned, finding the situation a bit peculiar. "Isn't that a bit strange?"

"The HR team had informed us that we could only terminate her employment after completing the inquiry," Pranjal explained.

"Okay, okay. What was the accusation against her?" Yohan pressed on.

"She was always taking long breaks and constantly bothering the admissions team for unnecessary data," Pranjal explained. "For example, she wanted to know the rankings of multiple users, their contact information, and other details that were not relevant to her job."

"And that was a problem because...." Sukumar prompted, wanting to understand Pranjal's perspective.

"I mean, her job was to work on campaigns to bring in new leads, not analyse how existing customers were performing," Pranjal said. "It's important for a marketer to focus on the marketing funnel and lead generation, not individual customer performance."

"It's very reassuring to hear you refer to these students as customers, Mr. Pranjal," Ila couldn't help but make a pointed remark, taking a dig at the coaching industry as a whole.

"I speak the language my job demands, ma'am," Pranjal replied confidently.

"Even if the purpose of your job is to secure a safer future for the children?" Ila challenged him.

"Ma'am, that's the purpose of education. I am marketing a product that can help them reach that future," Pranjal defended his perspective.

Sukumar found the banter between Pranjal and Ila amusing. He couldn't help but notice their similar mechanical approach to things. "Oh my God. There are two of them," he muttered to Yohan, sharing his observation.

"Shut up, *anna*, and focus," Yohan scolded Sukumar, surprised to see Ila getting sidetracked for once.

"Is this how machines flirt?" Sukumar couldn't resist making a quick joke.

Yohan ignored the comment and cleared his throat to redirect the conversation to the matter at hand. "Okay, Pranjal, why do you think Zulekha was after that information?" he inquired.

"Maybe to sell it to a rival company or… umm, she was really into mental health, being a yoga instructor. Perhaps she wanted to conduct some stress management coaching for some extra bucks. I don't know," Pranjal provided an answer for every possibility.

"Hmm. Can you guide us to some of Zulekha's colleagues or friends in the organisation?" Yohan realised that further questioning Pranjal would only lead to a rant by a disgruntled boss.

"Sure," Pranjal responded, dialling a number on his phone and calling a woman into his cabin. "Amita will be right here," he referred to his colleague.

"*Anna*, why don't you go and chat with Amita," Yohan instructed Sukumar. "If you don't mind, Mr. Pranjal."

"You have the COO's permission, so please go ahead," Pranjal agreed.

Sukumar quickly rushed outside to meet Amita, hoping she could provide further information about Zulekha. He needed to piece together the puzzle surrounding her mysterious connections. Meanwhile, Yohan excused himself from the meeting with Pranjal, feeling a strong urge to investigate further. He headed towards the entrance, approaching the security personnel for some insights. With a few questions answered, Yohan made his way to the designated area outside the building. This particular spot, known as the smoking area, was where Pranjal mentioned Zulekha frequently spent her time.

Yohan conversed with the individuals present in the smoking area, hoping to gather any useful information. The tranquil atmosphere, surrounded by lush green plants, provided a sense of solace amidst the bustling office environment. Employees frequented this spot to relieve their stress during breaks, making it a potential source of valuable insights.

Meanwhile, Ila continued her discussion with Pranjal in the meeting room, determined to extract more details about the investigation involving Zulekha.

"Pranjal, can you provide me with the information, regarding the inquiry against Zulekha?" Ila inquired, trying to break through his guarded responses.

"All I know is that she was leaking some information. That's the extent of my knowledge," Pranjal responded, remaining cautious.

Undeterred, Ila persisted, posing multiple questions in various formats, hoping to uncover any useful leads from the employee.

As the conversation continued, Ila's phone suddenly vibrated, drawing her attention. It was a message in their shared group chat. Sukumar's text displayed a sense of excitement and intrigue: "Guys, I think we have a very solid lead. This is a very good connection."

Chapter 9
BREAKTHROUGH LIES IN THE EYES OF THE INVESTIGATOR

After days of relentless research, Adinarayan managed to establish contact with a disgruntled former employee of InfoEdge Analytica, the political consulting firm accused of selling user data to AhaLife. The woman, Vani Vilas, had been terminated from her job in the aftermath of the controversy. Seeking a discreet location for their meeting, they decided to convene in Carter Road in Bandra, a bustling area teeming with joggers, walkers, families, musicians, and countless people from all walks of life. It was a place where interested players met and engaged in chess matches.

Adinarayan and Vani occupied one of the chess stands at Carter Road, finding solace amidst the lively atmosphere surrounding them. The constant flow of activity gave them a veil of anonymity, shielding their discussion from prying eyes and ears.

Sitting across the chessboard, Adinarayan initiated the conversation, "Thank you for meeting me, Vani. Your insights into InfoEdge Analytica could prove invaluable in my investigation."

Visibly cautious but intrigued, Vani responded, "I'm still shocked by what happened and how the company handled it.

I'm willing to share what I know, but I need assurance that my identity will be protected."

Adinarayan nodded understandingly, assuring her, "Rest assured, Vani. Your confidentiality is of utmost importance to me. We want to shed light on the truth and hold those responsible accountable."

"So InfoEdge had multiple clients, including a lot of prominent parties in the country," Vani stated, her voice laced with intrigue. "You're a journalist, and you know that elections in India are not won solely through on-ground physical campaigns, right?"

Adi, a journalist himself and an avid observer of political dynamics, nodded in agreement. "Of course. The world doesn't know the majority of things that happen behind the scenes during elections."

"But for the upcoming Assam elections, they decided to work with Mr. Anup Baruah," Vani revealed, her voice carrying a hint of significance.

Adi's face contorted with disbelief as he processed the revelation. "You mean Anup Baruah of the Assam Tiger Liberation Force?" he asked, visibly upset by the connection.

Assam, one of the seven states in India's Northeast, had been embroiled in a militant separatist movement since 1979. Unlike the conflicts in Kashmir or even Punjab, the uprising in Assam had received little media attention domestically and internationally. The origins of the conflict can be traced back to the tensions between the native indigenous Assamese people and the Indian Government, stemming from allegations of neglect and a range of political, social, cultural, and economic issues, along with increasing levels of illegal immigration from Bangladesh. The violence in the region has resulted in more than 30,000 deaths so far.

"Why would they work with someone who has separatist tendencies? I mean, Baruah intends to have an independent

Assam, which is dangerous," Adi questioned, his concern evident.

"Well, the majority of the people in Assam do not subscribe to or agree with a separate statehood. The public doesn't seem to have much sympathy for these separatist forces," Vani explained. "For any political party, the people's emotions are their biggest strength. InfoEdge was tasked with the responsibility of building the movement and enhancing the image of the separatist cause."

"And how was AhaLife useful in all this?" Adi probed further.

"AhaLife had a massive user base in Assam. InfoEdge wanted to create Assam-based influencers, who would then disseminate content promoting the cause. Utilising neutral voices would help them shape public opinion about the movement," Vani clarified.

Adi's mind raced as he processed the information. The intricate plan orchestrated by InfoEdge and its collaboration with AhaLife had far-reaching implications for the upcoming elections in Assam. He knew that the manipulation of public sentiment through influencers and carefully crafted content posed a serious threat to the democratic process and the stability of the region. The revelation about the Assam Tiger Liberation Force (ATLF) and its collaboration with InfoEdge and AhaLife added a new layer of complexity to the investigation surrounding his wife's death. Memories of the story he had previously worked on resurfaced, reminding him of the depth of the separatist movement and the turmoil it had caused in Assam. He recalled George Alfred's book, which delved into the manipulation of data by political parties in India and how AhaLife's content was tailored for different elections. Adi couldn't help but wonder if this revelation was one of Alfred's findings for his next book. If it were, it would undoubtedly ignite a different controversy altogether.

"Vani, do you have any idea about George Alfred's disappearance?" Adi inquired, his voice filled with anticipation.

Vani paused for a moment, contemplating her response. "Of course, I'm aware of him and his book," she replied. "But if you're asking whether I leaked the information to him for his book, then no. My involvement in this entire affair is far more serious and significant than what Alfred's book covers."

"But Alfred went missing when he was about to release his second book that may have contained this information," he said. "Would you be able to find out who Alfred's source is?" Adi pressed.

Vani pondered for a moment, contemplating the potential avenues she could explore. "I have connections with a few people at AhaLife," she offered, her voice laced with sincerity. "Let me see if I can put you in touch with them. They might have some information that could help us."

****

At the CBI quarters in Delhi, the team quickly gathered in Yohan's cabin to discuss the new connection Sukumar had uncovered. Ila and Yohan sat attentively as Sukumar began to share his findings.

"So I was talking to Amita, and among many things, she mentioned that Zulekha, during one of their sessions at a house party, revealed that she knew Samar Singh Randhawa very well," Sukumar began.

"Knew him as in?" Ila inquired.

"Apparently, before heading to the party at a colleague's house, Zulekha wanted to stop by her place and change. It was the first and only time that Amita saw Zulekha's apartment, and there was a photo on the wall featuring Zulekha and Samar Singh," Sukumar relayed the details he had gathered from Amita.

"She must have asked about their relationship. What did Zulekha say?" Yohan probed further.

"According to Amita, Zulekha mentioned that she used to be Samar's yoga instructor," Sukumar answered.

"Wait a minute. Based on our information, Zulekha never spent significant time in Mumbai, except for a few short visits. Similarly, Samar never spent much time in Delhi. So how did this yoga connection come about?" Yohan raised a valid point.

"Perhaps they had online sessions?" Ila hypothesised.

"Why would a celebrity opt for online sessions? He could easily hire someone to come to his house," Yohan countered. "And, more importantly, Zulekha passed away in 2019, before the era of widespread online classes."

"Yeah, that's true," Ila agreed, contemplating Yohan's thoughts. "What are you hinting at, Yohan?"

"There's a massive amount of information and some strong connections between the murders, but I feel like we're missing something that ties it all together," Yohan mused, his mind immersed in deep analysis.

"Did you gather any additional information from Amita, Sukumar?" Ila inquired.

Sukumar replied, "Amita mentioned that Zulekha seemed disinterested in her job and more focused on helping students who didn't clear the entrance exams. She had a strong desire to reach out to them and provide support. Brighter Tutorials perceived this as intrusive and crossing boundaries."

"Yeah, even from Pranjal's discussion, it's evident that Zulekha had a genuine interest in mental health," Ila confirmed, connecting the dots.

Sukumar turned to Yohan, asking, "What do you think we should do next?"

Yohan pondered for a moment before responding, "I believe there's a place where we can find more answers."

"Where?" Sukumar inquired.

"So, Amita mentioned that she discovered Zulekha's connection to Samar through a photo in her house," Yohan began, "… although it may not be her house anymore. Ila, why don't you investigate further into her family, find out where her belongings are, and see if we can uncover more clues?"

"Okay, Yohan. Anything specific you are going after?" Ila sensed that Yohan had a specific plan in mind.

Yohan nodded, his eyes focused. "Yes, I want to reopen Samar Singh's case file. But before that, I think it's crucial for us to obtain Zulekha's old phone number. I want to trace the calls she made to the students she was helping."

"Do you think those calls hold any significant information?" a doubtful Sukumar asked.

"The possibilities are always endless, *anna*," Yohan smiled.

***

Given Sukumar's resourcefulness, gaining access to Zulekha's next of kin wasn't a Herculean task. The CBI Sub-Inspector knew the right phone calls to make and secured the necessary access. Based on his information, Zulekha's belongings were sent to her parent's house in Defence Colony, a posh residential area in South Delhi. In the 1990s, it had been primarily occupied by army personnel and had retained its quiet charm, with bungalows housing families.

"Man, this place has had a fascinating history," Yohan remarked, peering out of the back window and admiring the area he had watched grow as he grew up. Yohan had spent his childhood in Sainik Farms, another prestigious and controversy-ridden neighbourhood in Delhi. The area, often called the 'foreign country' closest to Delhi by the media due to its magnificent mansions reminiscent of Malibu, housed many elites, including Yohan's industrialist father.

"Our sir is in a mood to give us a history lesson," Sukumar chuckled, glancing back at Ila from the front seat.

Smiling, Yohan clarified, "No, you guys. This place has witnessed an interesting growth."

"This Defence Colony was set up in 1947 as an aftermath of India's partition. It was established as a settlement for serving Indian military officers who had to leave their homes on the other side of the newly drawn border in Muslim-majority Pakistan. The land was allocated by the newly independent Indian Government to provide a new home for these officers and their families.

Even in the 1990s, Defence Colony retained its charm with its picturesque bungalows boasting lovely front gardens. There were quiet lanes with minimal traffic, primarily occupied by retired military officers and their families. To supplement their pensions, many of these retirees rent out a portion of their houses to young tenants who came to the city in search of work. Commonly the rental accommodations in Defence Colony was the 'barsati'. These were one or two small rooms, along with a kitchen space and bathroom, constructed on the rooftops of the houses. They were built initially as a space for domestic help, but these barsatis, with their spacious terraces, became popular among young Indians and budget-conscious foreigners who came to the city for work.

"Then a wave of modernisation swept through Delhi, resulting in changes to the city's building regulations," Yohan explained, concluding his history lesson. The driver parked the car outside the residential building in B block, where Zulekha's family lived, marking their arrival.

"Delhi witnessed a transformation as these bungalows were converted into condominiums, attracting outside buyers who were willing to pay higher prices," Yohan continued, emphasising the bustling nature of the present-day Defence Colony.

As they stepped out of the car and approached the building, Yohan's words lingered in the air, painting a picture of the neighbourhood's evolution. The team climbed the stairs with purpose, reaching the first floor where Zulekha's family resided.

Yohan took a deep breath and pressed the doorbell, the sound echoing through the corridor. They waited patiently, anticipation building with each passing second. Finally, the door creaked open, revealing an elderly woman with a kind smile.

"Good afternoon, ma'am," Yohan greeted politely. "We are from the CBI, investigating a case related to your daughter, Zulekha. May we speak with you?"

The woman's smile faded slightly as she looked at the team, concern and curiosity evident in her eyes. She hesitated for a moment before stepping aside and gesturing for them to come in.

"Please, come inside," she invited them, her voice tinged with a mix of apprehension and hope. The team entered the modestly furnished living room, taking in the family photographs adorning the walls and the faint aroma of home-cooked meals lingering in the air.

"I'm Zulekha's mother, Farida," the woman introduced herself, her voice trembling slightly. The sudden thought of her daughter made her a tad bit uncomfortable, and tears rolled out of her eyes.

Yohan empathetically reassured her, saying, "We understand your worries, Mrs. Farida. We have been investigating what happened to Zulekha when she disappeared. We think there might be important connections that can help us understand more."

Mrs. Farida's eyes filled with tears, a mix of sadness and hope. "Oh, Zulekha…. She was such a bright and determined girl. Always eager to help others. I never thought I would lose her like this."

Yohan's heart went out to her, feeling the depth of her pain. He gently reached out and held Mrs. Farida's trembling hand, offering a comforting presence, "We are here for you, Mrs. Farida. We share your sorrow and are committed to unravelling the truth behind Zulekha's untimely fate. We want justice for her and will tirelessly pursue every lead to bring closure to this painful chapter."

Overwhelmed by sadness and hope, Mrs. Farida struggled to regain her composure. "I have missed her every day for the past three years. The void she left in my heart is indescribable. Please, bring me answers… bring me some solace."

Ila, deeply moved by the raw emotions filling the room, spoke softly, "We promise you, Mrs. Farida, we will do everything in our power to get her justice."

With a heavy sigh, Mrs. Farida nodded, her tear-stained face reflecting determination, "I will do whatever I can to assist you."

Sukumar looked around the house, taking in the neatly arranged furniture that perfectly complemented the television and the clock hanging at the hall's centre. The walls were adorned with numerous pictures of Zulekha and her parents, clearly indicating that she was their only daughter. Among them were photos of Zulekha's father, proudly wearing his military uniform and standing with his team.

"So, Zulekha's dad was in the army, huh?" Sukumar asked, curious to learn more.

"Yes, *beta.* Lieutenant General Ansari Ali Siddiqui of the Assam Regiment," Zulekha's mother replied, her voice momentarily gaining strength as she recalled her husband's military career.

Yohan, who had a good knowledge of history and Indian politics, was familiar with various military regiments in the country, including the Assam Regiment. He knew it was one of the prestigious regiments, having been established in the 1940s and having participated in significant conflicts like World War II and Operation Vijay during the Kargil War.

Realising that the regiment extensively recruited from the Northeastern states, Yohan sought clarification from Zulekha's mother, "So, was he from Assam or…?"

"He was from Shillong." Farida, being a military wife, understood the significance of the question. "But when Zulekha was young, we lived in various places across the Northeast; Assam too."

"Oh, wow. And why did Zulekha choose marketing as a career?" Sukumar inquired.

"She was always fascinated by the army, like her father, but she couldn't pursue it. After that, every job she took was a compromise. Marketing, yoga, journalism, teaching, and so on," Farida explained.

"Ah, so she also worked as a journalist and a teacher. That's great, *ma'am*," Ila chimed in, hoping to gather more insights.

"Yes, she did. Before we moved to Delhi, she worked as a teacher in her father's village in Shillong after she failed the army exam. She also worked with a newspaper in Dibrugarh in Assam. She loved the Northeast. And so do I," Farida reminisced.

"But you're originally from Delhi, right, madam?" Sukumar double-checked.

"Yes, *beta*," Farida confirmed. Yohan and Ila couldn't understand why the lady referred to Sukumar as "*beta*" and not them, but they brushed it off and continued with their questioning.

"*Maa*, can you give us the details of the school and newspaper where she worked? Do you have any articles?" Sukumar inquired.

"Sure, *beta*. I might have those in her box. Should I go look for it?" Farida offered, wanting to assist in any way she could.

"In a while, *maa*. Meanwhile, can you tell me when she worked in Shillong and Assam?" Sukumar asked further.

"Zulekha worked in Assam from 2015 to 2016 and in Shillong from 2016 to 2018," Farida recalled the timeline accurately.

"And were you with her during that time?" Yohan questioned.

"No, no. My husband passed away in 2010 after his retirement, and I've been in Delhi since 2005," Farida explained.

"So, how old was Zulekha when she started working in Assam? Was it her first job?" Yohan inquired, trying to piece together her career timeline.

"Yes, she failed the exam in 2014, and in 2015, she started her first job as a Yoga teacher in Shillong," Farida shared, reminiscing about her daughter's journey. "So she must have been 23 when she started in 2015."

"Ma'am, to which corps or regiment did she apply?" Yohan probed further.

"She applied to the Army Ordnance Corps, I believe. Not sure, though," Farida responded.

Yohan, familiar with the subject, added, "The Army Ordnance Corps (AOC) is an active corps, responsible for providing material and logistical support during war and peace. Since 1992, they have also started inducting women for these roles."

Ila knew about it and subtly reminded Yohan, "We know, boss."

Yohan had an apologetic look on his face as his behaviour was a borderline mix of know-it-all and mansplaining. The investigating team, particularly Yohan, was consumed with multiple thoughts as they delved deeper into Zulekha's life. However, there were still many missing pieces of the puzzle to connect.

"*Maa*, do you have any idea why she left all of that and joined Brighter?" Sukumar probed, searching for possible connections.

Farida replied, her voice emanating love, "She simply wanted to stay with me in Delhi. I also felt relieved but never asked her to let go of her dreams just because I was alone. I am a soldier's wife and know how to survive." Farida's words and unwavering confidence deeply resonated with Ila, who wished for more women to support each other, particularly their daughters, in pursuing their ambitions rather than succumbing to the imaginary 'code of conduct' imposed by patriarchal norms.

"Did she mention anything unusual about Brighter Tutorials?" Ila pressed further.

"We never really discussed work. Although, I noticed she made calls to students even after work hours," Farida recollected.

"Did she meet any of these students in person?" Sukumar inquired.

"I don't think so. I'm not sure, but I believe all the students she spoke to were not in Delhi," Farida tried her best to recall every detail, knowing that any information might prove useful.

"Do you have any knowledge about the locations or places these students were from?" Yohan sensed that any piece of information could potentially lead to a breakthrough.

"No, *beta*. I have no idea." Yohan didn't get an answer, but at least he finally got that '*beta*' tag that had been reserved just for Sukumar so far. He glanced at his watch, realising time was running short as they needed to brief Director Verma soon. To expedite the process, he asked, "*Maa*, would it be alright if Ila goes through Zulekha's belongings? We can continue our conversation in the meantime."

"Of course," Farida agreed readily. She quickly took Ila to Zulekha's room, where several boxes containing her belongings were stored. The room remained decorated and maintained as if the lady's departed daughter still lived there. Ila couldn't help but feel a lump in her throat, witnessing the strength and resilience of the elderly woman amidst these tumultuous times.

As Farida returned to the living room where the other two investigators were waiting, Yohan swiftly resumed questioning. He took a file from Sukumar's hands containing a photo of Mekhala and pointed towards the picture.

"*Maa*, do you know if Zulekha knew this lady?" Yohan asked immediately.

Farida shook her head, indicating she had no idea who the woman in the photo was.

Sukumar joined in, curious about another aspect, "How did Zulekha know Samar Singh Randhawa, the actor?"

"Oh, Samar. They met through an old friend," Farida replied.

Yohan's interest was piqued by the mention of a name, "Who, *maa*?"

"His name is Siddharth, I think," Farida recalled, her memory a bit fuzzy. "He was a boy from Kerala."

"*Maa*, do you know anything else about this Siddharth or Zulekha's relationship with Samar?" Yohan pressed for more information, hoping to uncover something significant.

"No, *beta*, I don't know much. I believe Siddharth was an IT employee or something," Farida offered the limited details she had.

Yohan quickly turned to Sukumar and made a gesture, silently conveying that he wanted him to investigate this person named Siddharth. Sukumar understood his boss's message and made a mental note to look into the matter.

Suddenly, Ila came rushing into the room, her eyes fixed on Yohan. She gestured urgently for him to divert his attention from the conversation with Farida. Yohan noticed her urgency and excused himself, making his way to Ila. Meanwhile, Sukumar continued to engage in conversation with Farida.

Entering the room with Ila, Yohan quickly asked, "What happened, Ila? What have you found?"

Ila had meticulously sorted and placed various items on Zulekha's bed. She picked up two particular items and showed them to Yohan. "This one seems unusual. Why was she researching this?" Ila's voice carried a hint of intrigue and curiosity.

Yohan took a closer look at the files, delving into the possibilities, realising that what Ila had discovered could be a significant breakthrough in the case. His focus sharpened as he absorbed the information before him.

Suddenly, Ila's attention shifted to the second item—a photo frame containing a picture of Zulekha with a certain individual whom both Yohan and Ila recognised. Yohan's and Ila's expressions transformed from curiosity to shock and disbelief. Time seemed to freeze as the weight of the revelation sank in.

At that moment, the investigation took an unexpected turn, hurtling down an uncharted path. The room was engulfed in an eerie silence, broken only by the sound of their racing hearts. The air crackled with a palpable tension as the investigators realised they were standing at the precipice of a dark secret, a hidden truth that could unravel everything they thought they knew.

Chapter 10
TOO MANY CONNECTIONS SPOIL THE GROWTH

"Viewers, today, the nation is in shock. We have lost one of our finest talents, Samar Singh Randhawa. He was found dead in his apartment in Andheri West. The police have deemed it a suicide. But why would a successful actor with a string of hits take such a drastic step? He was at the pinnacle of his career, enjoying fame, wealth, and the love of the people. This death raises mysterious questions. Was he under immense pressure from the industry? Is there favouritism or a hidden nexus in Bollywood that hinders outsiders from achieving the success they deserve?"

Yohan and his team sat glued to the TV screen, watching the reruns of various news channels covering Samar Singh's death from different angles. Amidst the multiple versions, one thing was certain—the circumstances surrounding the actor's demise were far from ordinary, despite appearances.

"Yohan, apart from the money credited to both their accounts, we have no concrete evidence connecting Mekhala to Samar," Sukumar felt a debate on the facts would lead to a better discussion.

"That's true, but we cannot ignore the fact that Zulekha had some knowledge or association with Samar. There's a potential link between Zulekha and Mekhala," Ila rebutted.

While the team deliberated, Yohan's mind delved into the other leads they had gathered from Zulekha's house. He was deep in thought, contemplating their significance.

"What's on your mind, Yohan? Are you thinking about the leads we discovered yesterday?" Ila inquired, knowing her boss well enough by now.

"Yes, exactly. Let's focus on the first lead for now. The second one requires a more meticulous approach," Yohan responded, his mind already strategizing their next steps.

Ila retrieved the file pertaining to the "first lead" that Yohan had mentioned. Zulekha had collected newspaper cuttings over several years, and one name stood out in most of them—Anup Baruah, the chief of Assam Tiger Liberation Force (ATLF), an organisation with separatist tendencies.

After the partition, independent India witnessed demands for separate states, and the Northeast was no exception. However, Assam was relatively peaceful compared to other regions, as the administration satisfied the majority of the people. The ATLF was known for carrying out extreme acts, such as kidnappings, targeting Hindi-speaking individuals in the region, attacking pipelines and government resources, and orchestrating bomb blasts to intimidate the state machinery.

"The early 1990s and the subsequent period were turbulent in Assam," Yohan spoke about the state's troubled history.

In most rural areas of Assam, life comes to a standstill after sunset. Doors are tightly latched, and even the cries of children are silenced with the fear of army soldiers arriving to enforce order. This situation was exacerbated in the early 1990s when brutal counter-insurgency operations aimed at quelling the separatist movement shook the entire state. The constant military intervention sowed deep mistrust among the Assamese population. It was during this tumultuous period that the Assam Tiger Liberation Force (ATLF) emerged, taking up arms to fight against the Indian military. The group garnered some support from the locals who felt victimised by the government's retaliatory actions, which also included tracking and attacking militants and their families. Exploiting these sentiments, the ATLF, led by Baruah, succeeded in recruiting many Assamese youths, further exacerbating conflicts with the Indian state."

"Why did these separatist tendencies emerge in the first place?" Sukumar asked, seeking to understand the roots of the issue.

"The origins can be traced back to the Partition of Bengal in 1905, but let's focus on just the recent history," Yohan responded, preparing to shed light on the complex dynamics.

Starting from the early 1970s, Assam has witnessed a significant influx of migrants from Bangladesh, with a large portion of them being illegal. Bangladesh, grappling with overpopulation, frequent floods, and resource scarcity, pushed people to seek a better life in India. This influx of migrants created a sense of fear among the Assamese population that they would eventually be outnumbered by 'foreigners,' endangering their cultural heritage, history, and traditions. The Assamese people demanded that the Indian government take action to address this issue, as the economic and socio-political implications of such massive migration were significant.

"In fact, in 1998, the then-Governor, Lt. Gen. (Retd) S. K. Sinha, wrote a report to President K.R. Narayanan, highlighting the impact of this migration on Assam," Yohan added, summarising the historical context.

ATLF is not the only separatist organisation, right? Sukumar checked.

"No, no. There are many more, but ATLF is the most dangerous and often orchestrates acts of terror, unlike the others."

What started as a simple murder case is now a complex one with national-level issues," Ila weighed in.

If it wasn't complex, why would we have been called?" Sukumar's words sounded as if he was congratulating himself and patting his back.

"Alright, let's focus, everyone. We need to understand why Zulekha was tracking Anup Baruah and the ATLF during her time as a journalist in Assam," Yohan urged, bringing the team's attention back to the crucial task at hand.

"What if it wasn't Brighter Tutorials she was after, but Anup Baruah all along?" Ila contemplated an alternative perspective.

"Exactly, we still haven't found any concrete connection between Anup and the others," Sukumar agreed.

Just then, Yohan's phone rang, causing Sukumar and Ila to fall silent. They knew that every phone call from this point forward could hold crucial information, especially considering the various leads they had been following. Yohan answered the call and listened intently. Within seconds, his expression changed. Wrinkles creased his forehead as he processed the gravity of the information.

As the call ended, a concerned Sukumar inquired, "What happened, boss?"

Yohan took a moment before responding, "I had asked our team to trace Siddharth, the individual Farida mentioned as the link between Zulekha and Samar."

"Yes," Sukumar and Ila replied in unison.

"His full name is Siddharth Mahadevan, and he works as an HR consultant for multiple MNCs," Yohan revealed.

"So, can we meet him right away, then?" Ila asked eagerly.

Yohan's next words dampened their spirits, "That's the problem. He is no longer alive."

A collective sigh filled the room, knowing that another potential connection had reached a dead end.

"And guys, he died in 2021," Yohan continued, providing more details. "And you know what that means?"

"Four murders in four years? Zulekha in 2019, Samar in 2020, Siddharth in 2021, and Mekhala in 2022," Ila concluded, the gravity of the situation sinking in.

"If all these incidents are connected, then we're dealing with a truly perplexing angle," Yohan spoke, his attention turning to the evidence board, realising the need to pin more names and angles to it.

⁂⁂

Yohan's heart raced as he switched on his phone after landing at Mumbai International Airport, only to be greeted by 17 missed calls. Seeing Sukumar, seated a few seats ahead on the flight, flash his mobile screen, indicating that he too had missed calls, heightened Yohan's concern. Director Verma's distress message read, *Check the news asap. Find out how this happened*, and added to the urgency of the situation.

Grabbing their cabin luggage, the team members hurried toward the exit gate. On the way, Yohan quickly turned on YouTube on his phone, eager to discover what had transpired. As the screen lit up, he was taken aback by what he saw.

The news anchor of News Now prepared himself for a debate and introduced the crime reporter, Shweta Sinha, who had broken the exclusive on the CBI investigation. "So, Shweta, you broke the exclusive with your latest article online," the news anchor said. "Can you repeat it for our viewers? Ladies and gentlemen, please listen to Shweta and decide for yourself."

Shweta began to share the information she had received: "Well, I got a tip regarding the investigation that the CBI team is now looking into the death of a Delhi-based marketing employee as part of the Mekhala investigation. So, the case is…"

Before Shweta could finish her sentence, the anchor abruptly interrupted her, eager to assert his viewpoint. "See, viewers, the CBI investigation is going off track and not focusing on the murder of Mekhala. This is sheer negligence of duty."

Sukumar, who detested the anchor's self-proclaimed representation of the Republic of India, shook his head in disdain. He couldn't help but resent how the anchor used his responsible platform to peddle sensationalised content and manipulate the facts.

Yohan watched Shweta as she spoke about the investigation's direction. Although relieved she didn't subscribe to the anchor's narrative, he couldn't shake off his frustration that she had made their investigation public in the media. Feeling a sense of urgency, he immediately sent a WhatsApp message to Shweta, *Shweta, please call me when you see this. It's urgent.*

As they hurried towards the sleek black car, Sukumar's eyes darted between his phone and Ila and Yohan, who were briskly leading the way. He quickened his pace to catch up with them, excitement evident in his voice. "Boss, Ila, I have the call records of Mekhala, Zulekha, and Samar. Siddharth's, I'll get in a day or two," Sukumar informed, trying to keep up with their pace.

"Oh, brilliant, *anna.* Start analysing it from the car itself. With this media leak, we need to proceed faster," Yohan instructed, with a sense of haste in his voice.

Sukumar nodded, his face beaming with pride, "Yes, yes. I'm way ahead of you, boss. I've already instructed the team to comb through the records, highlighting any common numbers between the three suspects and flagging any unusual calls they come across." His efficiency and meticulousness were evident

"Yohan, we still have to explore Samar's angle, Siju, Siddharth and also plan a trip to Assam to investigate Zulekha further," Ila began laying out the team's plan of action.

"Before all that, I want to know who leaked the news to the media," Yohan expressed his concern, his eyes glued to his phone as he checked for any response from Shweta.

"In that case, I will discreetly meet Samar's old house staff, manager and others to see if I can get more information. I've already lined up a few meetings," Ila shared her plan, determined to dig deeper into the matter.

"Great! Take another vehicle and proceed directly. We can't waste a single moment." Yohan expressed his confidence in Ila's abilities as he and Sukumar were about to enter the waiting car. Sukumar, already lost in his phone, busily assessed the Excel sheet with the call logs and data, focusing on finding any significant patterns.

Finally, Yohan's phone came to life – the long-awaited call flashing Shweta's name on the screen. A mix of relief and frustration washed over him as he answered the call, "Hey, Shweta, you could have told me once before publishing," he expressed, a hint of irritation in his voice.

"Hey, Yohan, you're the one who said that we'll keep personal and professional separate."

"I know, Shweta. But this is going to affect our investigation."

"I'm sorry, but I'm not sorry. I was just doing my job."

"Please don't get me wrong. I'm not interfering in your work in any manner. I just need one small help."

"Tell me."

"Who gave you the information about Zulekha?"

"Yohan, you know that I can't reveal my source," Shweta's voice was laced with the weight of journalistic ethics.

"Shweta, this is serious. Your information will help this case. At the end of the day, you also want a solution as a crime reporter," Yohan reasoned, hoping to appeal to Shweta's sense of justice.

"But, Yohan, a source is a source," Shweta hesitated, torn between her duty as a journalist and the potential impact of her revelation.

"I know. But this is now standing in the way of delivering justice to two women," Yohan acknowledged the complexity of the situation, keeping his cards close to his chest, withholding the information about Samar's angle, knowing that it wasn't out yet.

Shweta fell into a sea of silence, deep in contemplation. She weighed the pros and cons, realising that it would be against her professional ethics and potentially even the law to withhold information that could contribute to securing justice. Eventually, she caved, knowing the importance of the moment. She finally revealed a name that made Yohan's face grow more serious.

"With a hint of disbelief, he asked to confirm, "Are you sure, Shweta?"

"Damn sure I am," Shweta affirmed, her voice unwavering. "And you owe me a big one now, Yohan."

Yohan nodded on his end of the line, acknowledging Shweta's request. He understood the significance of what she had just done, knowing that it takes tremendous trust and courage for journalists to reveal their source. "Yes, I will return the favour", he promised.

****

As the evening shadows crept into the CBI guesthouse in Vile Parle, the atmosphere crackled with intensity. Sukumar sat in the cosy living area, deeply engrossed in analysing the intricate web of call records. His eyes darted across the screen, diligently tracing the connections, determined to unearth any hidden clues.

In the adjacent room, Yohan sat at a sleek glass desk, bathed in the soft glow of the overhead lights. The case files sprawled before him, like a labyrinth waiting to be deciphered. He combed through Siddharth Mahadevan's career history, the HR consultant who had recently emerged as the latest one in the murder series they were investigating. The weight of the case bore down on him, but he remained determined.

As Yohan delved into the case file, a world of possibilities unfurled before him. The pages whispered tales of Siddharth Mahadevan's professional journey, unveiling a captivating personality - Siddharth was a master of campus placements, a trailblazer who traversed the length and breadth of the country in pursuit of talent. The details painted a vivid picture of Siddharth's tireless efforts, his travels taking him from the bustling streets of Mumbai to the vibrant campuses of Kolkata and the enigmatic landscapes of Assam. He had woven a tapestry of connections, cultivating relationships with principals, deans, and placement coordinators in his quest to secure stellar opportunities for ambitious students.

The file spoke of Siddharth's relentless dedication, his fingerprints were found in the annals of universities, where he meticulously sought out the crème de la crème of academia. He had a successful track record of placing bright minds in prestigious Global & National MNCs and innovative Indian Startups.

Ila was still outside and conducting her inquiries related to Samar's case and had yet to return to the guest house.

"How's it going, *anna*?" Yohan checked on Sukumar's progress.

"There are a few surprises, but I'm still hunting," Sukumar replied, stifling a yawn that hinted at his exhaustion from countless travels and on-ground investigations. "How's yours going, boss?"

"I've been browsing through the top MNCs and universities that Siddharth worked with,"

"Anything interesting, boss?"

"I'm assessing the frequency of Siddharth's association with these entities, creating a list of the top ones he worked with."

"What's the objective, boss?"

"To see if there's any pattern there."

"And how would this pattern help?"

"Once I have the top ones, I want to map and see if any of the students that Zulekha tried to reach out to study in any of these institutes. If there's a connection, it might shed light on the motive or potential links between Siddharth and Zulekha."

Sukumar's curiosity heightened, he was eager to understand Yohan's hypothesis. "But what is your hypothesis? And we don't have the list of students Zulekha reached out to."

"For that, we can just trace the students' history and see if they were associated with Brighter Tutorials in any manner."

"Yeah, that makes sense. But have you got any leads?"

Yohan grinned, flipping through his notes eagerly. "Yes, indeed! Siddharth has facilitated placements in numerous MNCs and startups. However, when it comes to universities, there are seven that dominantly stand out among the others."

"Are they all Guwahati-based?"

"No, there are two from Assam, but three are located in Mumbai, and one each in Calcutta and Tamil Nadu."

"All private universities?"

Yohan nodded, his voice filled with affirmation, "Yeah, *anna.* It seems Siddharth had a keen interest in these institutions."

Sukumar's expression turned thoughtful as he contemplated the significance. "That's quite a substantial amount of data, boss. Do you want me to handle it?"

Yohan raised his hand, "I appreciate your willingness, Sukumar. But let me give it a shot. I want to dive into this task myself. You already have enough on your plate."

Sukumar's smile widened, a silent acknowledgement of Yohan's leadership style. He admired Yohan's dedication to leading from the front, never shying away from getting his hands dirty.

At this point, Ila walked into the guesthouse, looking extremely tired and worn out after her exhaustingly long day. She dropped her bag and hurriedly gulped down water from the jug placed on the dining table in the living room. Yohan and Sukumar exchanged glances, noticing her fatigued state, and decided to give her a moment to freshen up before bombarding her with questions.

Finally finding her voice, Ila let out a sigh of disappointment, "Guys, please tell me you have something concrete."

Sukumar, concerned, inquired, "What happened, Ila? Whom did you manage to meet?"

"I met Samar's manager and his former house help," Ila replied promptly.

"What did you gather from them?" Yohan followed up.

"Mostly, it was routine stuff..." Ila began to paint a picture of Samar's activities in the week leading up to his death. He had a regular gym visit every morning before heading to his office and preparing for his upcoming movies. Last week, he had meetings with two producers at their offices in Andheri West, wherc most production houses in Mumbai are located. He was also in the process of hiring an accent coach for one of his upcoming movies, so he interviewed 2 to 3 candidates. Additionally, he met up with his school friends on a Saturday evening for a night of alcohol, good food, and heartfelt conversations.

Ila's voice became more sceptical as she continued, "He even received his second dose of the COVID-19 vaccine that week. Would someone about to commit suicide do that?"

The pieces of the puzzle seemed to shift, challenging their assumptions and demanding a more thorough investigation. The room became a vortex of anticipation, each member of the team contemplating the significance of the new information.

"Ila, just read out Samar Singh's post-mortem report," Yohan requested.

Ila took a deep breath and proceeded to read aloud the crucial section of the case file. "According to the report, Samar was found unconscious and later declared dead based on the medical investigation. The preliminary evidence doesn't suggest any struggles or physical marks on the body, clearly negating the presence of any sort of manhandling or assault. Initial testing on the body indicates the use of painkillers, and an overdose is certain to have caused the death. The individual's body shows signs of exhaustion from lack of sleep, leading to the use of the medicine in higher quantities, ultimately resulting in his demise.

"No signs of an external entry, no body bruises. He was going about his business as usual. How did one of India's promising actors just lay down dead in his apartment one day?" a frustrated Ila exclaimed as the case was getting more intense by the day.

"I don't know how exactly Samar died, but his phone records do tell an interesting story," Sukumar shared, ready with some analysis.

"Yes, *anna*. You are the greatest. Just give me a breakthrough," Ila slipped out of her reserved character, praising Sukumar for providing a new piece of information in this puzzling case that has been a headache for the team.

"What do the call records suggest, anna?" Yohan asked, equally curious.

"So, of course, there have been calls to the manager, roommate, colleagues, etc. But there was a private number that he called multiple times over the span of three months," Sukumar revealed.

"And who does it belong to?" Ila inquired.

"Those records are not accessible at this point. I am on it," Sukumar assured his team.

"Anything similar in Zulekha or Mekhala's case?"

"That's the other thing. Samar and Zulekha have spoken in the past, as per their call records, before Zulekha's death. Now I have to look at Mekhala's call data from that time period because she was the last one alive," Sukumar clarified.

"But you did analyse Mekhala's latest calls, right?" Yohan asked.

"Yes, I did."

"Anything interesting there?" Ila chimed in.

"No, with Mekhala, I could trace calls to her authors and publisher. Right before her death, she called Adinarayan multiple times and even dropped him a message, but he never returned her calls or texted back," Sukumar added.

"Wait a minute, Adinarayan never picked up her calls or returned them?" Yohan picked up on the detail as he sat with the weight of something else on his mind.

"Yeah, but it isn't unusual for a wife to call or message her husband, right?" Sukumar cross-checked.

"No, but look at the frequency of the calls. This could also be a distress call, don't you think?" Ila also agreed.

"Her phone might still be in Kamble's custody. Ask him to check it right away and send us the content of those messages," Yohan urged, his intuition driving him to dig deeper into the matter.

Initially hesitant about the lead, Sukumar decided to give it a shot and stepped outside to make the call, hoping to uncover crucial information.

"Is there any connection we are missing, boss?" Ila inquired, her curiosity growing.

"Let's wait for Sukumar to return. Once he's back, I'll explain everything."

At that moment, Sukumar entered the room, his face etched with confusion, puzzlement, and a glimmer of hope. He rubbed his tired eyes, clearly affected by the long hours of investigation.

"What's with that face, Sukumar?" Yohan turned his attention to his teammate.

"Boss, you were right," Sukumar began, "… Mekhala's last message to Adinarayan was BOM 6324."

Ila couldn't help but smile, "Thank goodness. Unlike crime thriller movies, Mekhala didn't leave a cryptic clue for investigators to decipher."

"Indeed," Yohan agreed. "BOM indicates Bank of Mumbai, and '6324' seems to be a regular bank locker number. I'll inform the team to check it out."

Sukumar answered, assuring Yohan, "I'll take care of it, boss."

Yohan, deep in thought, silently nodded in acknowledgement. Ila, noticing his contemplative state, sensed an opportunity to bring up her earlier question.

"Boss, you mentioned there was something amiss. Now that Sukumar is back, could you share with us?"

"Yeah, boss. I also want to ask, why you're really behind Adinarayan? Have you developed a bias like him?" Sukumar asked, his voice tinged with accusation.

Yohan's eyes widened at the implication. He quickly responded, a hint of annoyance in his tone, "Of course not, guys. We should never let our personal biases influence our investigations. You know that."

Ila, sensing the tension in the room, interjected, "Sorry to bring it up again, boss, but this behaviour is unlike you. We're just trying to understand."

Yohan took a deep breath, collecting his thoughts before continuing, "Let me explain, Ila. Remember when I spoke to Shweta earlier today to inquire about her source for the article?"

Both Sukumar and Ila nodded in unison.

"It turns out," Yohan revealed, his voice laced with a mix of suspicion and confusion, "… the source was Adinarayan himself. He deliberately leaked the news to her."

The revelation hung in the air, leaving Ila and Sukumar perplexed. They struggled to comprehend the motive behind Adinarayan's actions and its connection to the unfolding case.

Chapter 11
DON'T COUNT YOUR SUSPECTS BEFORE THEY CRACK

Yohan sat at a small table in the bustling cafe, engrossed in Siddharth Mahadevan's case file. The information he uncovered painted a picture of a man who had experienced both tragedy and success. Siddharth's journey began at Madras Christian College, where he pursued a degree in Journalism. Afterwards, he worked as a marketing executive for a prominent multinational company in Delhi. However, after two years, he made a career shift, becoming an HR consultant specialising in placing candidates.

Based on his earlier analysis, he had discovered an intriguing pattern. Siddharth had a strong association with seven specific universities: Vellore Technology Institute, Bombay Technical School, Jaipal Law University, Guwahati Arts College, Tagore Institute of Arts and Sciences, Indrapuri University, and Buddha Institute of Commerce. It seemed that Siddharth focused on assisting students from these institutions in securing placements.

One particular aspect caught Yohan's attention—Siddharth's early life. The file revealed that Siddharth had tragically lost his parents at a young age, leaving him with no relatives. As a result, he was raised in a Muslim orphanage in

Malappuram, Kerala. The details added a layer of complexity to Siddharth's story, providing insight into the challenges he had overcome.

While Yohan immersed himself in the case file, Ila sat across from him, occasionally glancing at her watch. They were waiting for Siddharth's close friend, Hanif Aslam, who had agreed to meet them at the cafe in Bandra. Meanwhile, Sukumar was on a mission to unlock the mystery surrounding Mekhala's locker and was planning to meet a family friend residing in Mumbai.

The file, however, took a chilling turn as Yohan read about Siddharth's demise. Like Mekhala, Siddharth had met a tragic end, but it wasn't at his home. Instead, he perished in a devastating fire that engulfed a club in South Bombay where he had been partying with his friends. The incident didn't raise a lot of suspicion, especially considering the city's recent history of such fires.

"What do you think of the fire, Ila?"

"I am not sure, Yohan. It could be an accident. Why would anyone who wants Siddharth dead blow up a club?" Ila questioned, her voice tinged with uncertainty.

Yohan acknowledged her point with a thoughtful hum and immersed himself in Siddharth's case file.

Ila caught a man conversing with the entry gate steward, the same man they were waiting for. "Look, I think that's him," she whispered, pointing discreetly. Yohan followed her line of sight and confirmed that it was Hanif, Siddharth's close friend.

Raising his hand from a distance, Yohan caught Hanif's attention, prompting him to approach their table. "Hello, Mr. Yohan, Ms. Ila. I am Hanif," he introduced himself politely.

The investigators greeted Hanif and requested him to take a seat. Ila, having rehearsed her lines as a conversation starter, spoke up. "Mr. Hanif, if it's okay with you, we would like to begin with a few questions about Siddharth. We appreciate you taking the time to meet with us amidst your busy schedule."

Hanif nodded, displaying a calm demeanour, "Sure, please go ahead. I'm here to assist in any way I can."

"Since when did you know Siddharth?"

"I have known Siddhu since our time at the orphanage. We drifted apart after he went to college, but we started reconnecting when we both began working."

Yohan smiled inwardly at the mention of Siddhu, reflecting on how nicknames could vary across different regions of India. In North India, a Siddharth would most likely be referred to as Sid, whereas in Kerala, Siddhu would be more common.

The team identified Hanif from a Facebook photo posted by Siddharth, in which Hanif had been tagged. Even though the photo dated back to a year before Siddharth's untimely death, it was crucial to connect with Hanif, who was an IT professional in Mumbai.

Curiosity burning within him, Yohan continued the conversation. "What was Siddharth like, Hanif? Do you have any doubts regarding his death?"

"Doubts? Why would I have any doubts, sir?" Hanif's puzzled expression revealed his confusion. "He died in a fire accident. It was tragic."

Yohan leaned forward, sporting a serious face, "Sometimes accidents aren't as straightforward as they appear. We want to consider all possibilities and uncover the truth behind Siddharth's death. Your insights and any information you can provide might be crucial to our investigation."

Hanif's face turned pale as he absorbed the gravity of Yohan's statement. He was visibly tense, never having experienced such a serious situation before. The pressure weighed heavily on him, and it was evident in his demeanour.

Ila sensed the guardedness in Hanif's tone and intensified her efforts, "Please, Hanif, share whatever you can recall about Siddharth. Something unusual that stood out for you?"

Hanif took a moment to collect his thoughts, his gaze fixed on a distant point as he delved into his memories, "Siddhu… he carried a deep sense of disappointment because of the loss of his parents. He always felt like their death left him with no name or recognition in this world. It pushed him to work hard and create a name for himself."

"Why is it that we often remember and speak only about the admirable qualities of someone only after they have passed away?" Ila questioned, hungry for more information.

"One thing I remember – he hated people being exploited, especially children. It must be because we all had nobody growing up," Hanif added, his voice filled with sadness and determination.

Yohan connected the dots, "Is that why he left marketing and moved to HR, to help students get a better job and life?"

Hanif nodded, "Yes, exactly. Siddharth wanted to make a difference and ensure that young individuals like himself had a chance to succeed. He believed in giving them opportunities he never had."

Ila's curiosity grew, "Do you know why he moved to Guwahati?"

Hanif explained, "He used to travel there for work and developed a fondness for the place. Since he had a job that required frequent travelling, he decided to settle down in a city he genuinely liked. And, Yohan sir, to answer your question… I remember him saying that he finally had a job that gave meaning to his life."

As Hanif spoke, a few tears trickled down his cheeks, reflecting his emotional connection with Siddharth.

Yohan sensed an angle worth exploring, "Hanif, do you think he might have picked fights with individuals who exploited or misled children?"

Hanif pondered for a moment. "Not that I know of, but it does sound like something Siddharth would do. Why, sir? I still can't comprehend how someone could kill a person like Siddharth."

Yohan's expression turned serious as he cautioned Hanif, "Hanif, keep this information to yourself. We're still investigating various possibilities. It may not be what we initially suspected."

Hanif nodded in understanding, his emotions still raw, "I understand, but we're talking about a passionate guy who loved his job. At one point, he even wanted to join the army."

The revelation caught Ila and Yohan off guard. They exchanged a meaningful glance, recognising the significance of this new information.

"He worked in the army?" Ila's eyes lit up with intrigue.

"No, he didn't. He couldn't clear the tests and was disappointed," Hanif clarified.

Yohan pressed further, "Hanif, are you absolutely sure about this?"

"Yes, sir."

In that pivotal moment, a flicker of determination ignited within Yohan's eyes. The connection between Zulekha's aspiration to join the army and Siddharth's similar ambition, despite both facing rejection, sparked a realisation in Yohan's mind. A sinister plot involving rejected army aspirants began to take shape in his thoughts.

***

There has to be a connection. Ila, find out if Samar and Mekhala also have a history of being rejected by the army.

This pattern needs to be confirmed before we proceed further," Yohan instructed Ila as they settled back at the guesthouse, waiting for Sukumar.

Ila nodded, her mind already racing with the task at hand, "Sure, boss. I'll dig into their backgrounds and see if there are any commonalities."

"What are you reading, by the way ?" she asked, as Yohan was meticulously studying.

Yohan's eyes never left the documents as he replied, "This is the report on the fire that broke out at the club where Siddharth died."

Ila's scepticism lingered, "You still think it wasn't just a regular fire? I mean, Mumbai has a history of such incidents."

Yohan glanced up from the files, "Ila, why don't you read this part?" he suggested, pointing to a specific section in the report.

The report read, *The forensic evaluation concluded that the fire's origin resulted from modifications made to the electrical components within the DJ panel. It is crucial to acknowledge that electrical wires possess specific capacities for safely carrying electrical currents, as these capacities depend on wire gauge or thickness. Overloading the wire with an electrical load surpassing its capacity initiates excessive current flow, generating heat. Such overheating of wires escalates the risk of insulation breakdown and potential fire hazards. In the case of the Elmore Social at Kamala Mills, substandard wires were employed, giving rise to the initial spark. Moreover, wires with inadequate gauge sizes failed to adequately manage the electrical load, resulting in excessive current flow and potential overheating. Consequently, this elevated electrical resistance, coupled with insufficient insulation, triggered sparks, electrical arcing, and subsequent ignition of nearby combustible materials, ultimately culminating in a substantial fire. Additionally, the investigation uncovered evidence indicating the escape of hydrofluorocarbons (HFCs) or hydrochlorofluorocarbons (HCFCs) from the air conditioning unit, which came into contact with an open flame, exacerbating the fire's severity.*

Analysing technical information wasn't Ila's strength. She turned to Yohan with a helpless look, "Okay, boss, you have to explain."

Yohan sported a smile, "See, the bad wires and inadequate insulation resulted in electrical arcing and short circuits. This ignited the DJ panel, causing the fire. And on top of that, an existing gas leak in the AC made the fire worse."

"Okay, but how is that suspicious?" Ila still didn't follow.

"For that, you need to see this report," Yohan handed her another file.

"This is…" Ila looked puzzled.

"Yes, this is the report from the fire at Mekhala's neighbour's house," Yohan handed over another paper, "… and read this portion carefully."

Ila began reading the report, *Upon a thorough investigation of the scene and forensic evaluation of the affected area, it was determined that the wiring of the karaoke machine exhibited significant deficiencies. The wiring utilised for the electrical connections within the machine proved to be substandard, thus failing to meet the necessary quality and safety standards. This substandard wiring posed a critical risk, as it could not adequately handle the electrical load required by the karaoke machine's components.*

The presence of inadequate wiring and the heightened electrical load demands imposed by the karaoke machine resulted in an escalation of current flow through the wires. Consequently, this amplified current flow increased susceptibility to electrical arcing and potential short circuits. Furthermore, it is noteworthy that a gas leak, likely originating from a household appliance, exacerbated the hazardous conditions, further intensifying the fire's magnitude.

"I see what you're saying, but I'm still struggling to pinpoint the exact connection," Ila admitted, sensing that

Yohan was onto something significant. She eagerly awaited his clarification.

Yohan took a moment to gather his thoughts, his eyes focused and determined, "Listen, Ila. These may appear to be two separate incidents, but the *modus operandi* remains consistent. In both cases, we have substandard wiring in external devices—the DJ panel at the club and the karaoke machine in Mekhala's adjacent house. The science behind the short circuits is identical. Moreover, we can't overlook the presence of a gas leak originating from an appliance, specifically the AC at the club. These fires were orchestrated, meticulously planned and executed."

Ila's face displayed a mix of shock and disbelief. The realisation that the murderer had gone to such lengths, orchestrating a large-scale fire to eliminate a single person, sent chills down her spine. However, amidst her astonishment, she couldn't help but feel a surge of pride for Yohan's brilliant mind. He had unravelled a crucial detail that could have easily gone unnoticed. Her admiration for her boss grew, and she couldn't help but swell with pride at his exceptional intelligence and deductive abilities.

"But, Yohan, I still have a doubt," Ila may not have possessed the technical knowledge, but she certainly had the inquisitive aptitude of an investigator. "I understand that causing an AC gas leak in a club would be relatively easy given the number of people and technicians present. However, orchestrating the same in a household AC would require significant effort. The outdoor units of most ACs are usually located outside and not easily accessible. So, how could the person behind the party have accomplished that?"

Yohan acknowledged Ila's question, appreciating her keen observation, "That's a good doubt, Ila. But it wasn't the AC."

"Then what was it?"

"It was most certainly the fridge," Yohan revealed confidently.

"How can you be so sure, boss?"

"Because the answer lies within the post-mortem reports of Surabhi and her husband," Yohan responded, referring to Mekhala's neighbours.

Ila stood still, her undivided attention fixed on Yohan as he took out the reports and pointed to a specific word mentioned within. "Look here," he began, "… their bodies exhibit clear signs of freon inhalation." He paused for a moment, allowing the information to sink in. "Freon, specifically R-134a, is the most commonly used refrigerant in fridges. It is typically located at the back of the device, next to the compressor."

Ila's face displayed a multitude of emotions—shock, surprise, and a tinge of disbelief. "Whoa, this is crazy, boss," she exclaimed, struggling to process the revelation.

Yohan continued, connecting the dots with confidence, "And the party organising team would have had easy access to the fridge, making it easy to introduce the lethal gas," he concluded.

"So we need to find the team that organised these parties and events and see if they are the same," Ila comprehended the next plan of action.

"I am already on it," Yohan confirmed. "By the way, the findings don't end there."

Ila, already overwhelmed with the latest revelation, wasn't ready for more but patiently waited for her team lead to delve deeper into his findings.

"In the meantime, I also retrieved Surabhi's information since she has had multiple interactions with Mekhala," Yohan began, turning the pages of his diary. "Turns out it wasn't just Surabhi who interacted with Mekhala."

Yohan pulled out the detailed phone records that Sukumar had sourced, and in Mekhala's call logs, there was one particular number circled in blue ink to distinguish it from the red inks of other calls.

"Whose number is this, boss?"

"It belongs to Anand Bhattacharya, Surabhi's husband," Yohan continued. "But that isn't the strange part."

"This is getting dramatic. You've caught Sukumar's fever of building things up."

"Haha, I am sorry. So these calls with Mekhala are long ones that have lasted for more than 30 minutes."

"But they are neighbours, so it shouldn't be that unusual, right?"

"Yeah, that is fine, but what makes it strange is that if you remember, Anand worked for a private bank, and it is the same bank from where Siju Sharatchandran, the educational businessman, had taken the loan and the scam that followed."

"This is an unending circle of connections and conspiracies," Ila sighed at the thought of an entirely new angle to follow up on.

"And Mekhala's author and journalist, Preetam Gowda, who exposed this, was preparing for the book. As per Anand's bank office records, Preetam met with Anand at his bank. So there is a strong possibility that Anand was one of his sources," Yohan unravelled the cobwebs of the mystery he had uncovered.

"So, Siju has a strong motive to eliminate Anand and Mekhala," Ila added.

"Exactly, and that could make Mekhala's murder an isolated one then. Because Siju has no connection with the others, at least till now," Yohan raised the questions that plagued his mind, even with the recent findings.

As the discussions proceeded, a visibly exhausted Sukumar entered, puffing and panting after a long day in the field. He had tirelessly traversed multiple locations in the pursuit of truth and followed up on leads. Sukumar's face showed signs of weariness, yet his eyes sparkled with satisfaction and anticipation. He placed his bag on the table and took a moment to catch his breath before recounting the day's events.

"*Anna*, please tell me your efforts have yielded something. Because you look like a tired and deflated person," Yohan tried to rile up Sukumar, who always loved a reason to be pumped up.

"Oh, I have a back full of pain and a mind full of data." Even in his most tired state, Sukumar's affinity for drama never ended.

"And does any of it connect to what we have captured so far?" a visibly tired Ila asked, silently praying for closure.

"*Konjam* patience, Ila madam," Sukumar said, regaining his breath.

"Tell us already, sir. Today has been a day of revelations and connections to the extent that I am praying that whatever you have found just helps us go in one direction instead of this multi-lane highway we are riding on," Ila pressed, eager for answers.

Sukumar took his phone from his pocket, slowly walked towards his colleagues, opened the gallery on it, and flashed a photograph forwarded to him by Mekhala's aunt. Upon seeing the photo, Yohan quickly grabbed the phone to take a closer look, while Ila snuck in through the crook of his shoulder to confirm. Their faces, clouded with surprise, shock and a mix of similar emotions, clearly indicated the gravity of the proof that Sukumar had produced before them.

"So, Zulekha and Mekhala both have individual pictures with this person," Yohan's hands felt soft, recognising the significance of this discovery. They had previously uncovered a photograph in Zulekha's house that raised curiosity, but this confirmed their wildest imaginations.

"What do we do now, boss?" Ila asked, her mind evaluating all angles.

"We do our job and question them. No matter who they are," Yohan stood firm, ready to face the new challenges that lay ahead in their journey towards solving this case. "But there's just one catch. We need to gather more evidence."

Chapter 12
A GOON AND HIS LOYALTY ARE SOON PARTED

"As per the location, he is currently inside the Saki Naka *chawl* area below the metro gate," Sukumar gave instructions on the phone, sitting with Circle Inspector Said Kamble in the police control room in Andheri East, which was less than five kilometres away from the Saki Naka *Chawl* area where Yohan and Ila were positioned.

After the new revelations, the team delved deep into entrepreneur Siju Sharatchandran and his close aides, including the businessman's personal secretary, Rita Khamboj. While analysing Rita's phone records and reviewing CCTV footage near a restaurant in Saki Naka, the team identified that she had called and met with a notorious rowdy in the area, Aleem Sulaiman. Aleem was known for his close proximity to individuals like politicians, industrialists, and businessmen. He was not a name that stirred fear among the locals since Mumbai police had successfully contained the perils of the underworld in the city of dreams. However, Aleem was recognised for his expertise in abductions, money recovery and other notorious activities, making him a useful asset for people like Siju Sharatchandran. The clandestine meeting between Rita and Aleem, a mere two days before the chilling abduction of Preetam Gowda, forged a connection too uncanny to ignore. The meticulously synchronised timing ignited an insatiable urge to delve deeper into Aleem's world, driven by the desperate need to uncover any link that could lead them closer to Preetam.

"You guys have to navigate carefully through the *chawl.* It is packed, and the roads are narrow," Sukumar continued to give instructions.

Yohan and Ila had their Bluetooth earpieces on as they listened to Sukumar. "*Anna*, I know what a *chawl* looks like. Give us more accurate information on his location." Yohan and Ila were dressed in casual attire, with Yohan wearing an untucked full-sleeve shirt and pants, while Ila had donned a salwar and even wore earrings, deviating from her usual appearance to blend in with the crowd. They had police backup stationed at various points in the *chawl* because this was a place where Aleem had a few henchmen scattered here and there, although it wasn't his regular turf, which lay farther away in the chawls of Kurla, closer to South Bombay. The team knew that capturing the goon here was their best chance to bring him in for questioning, and they couldn't afford to miss this opportunity by any means.

The narrow bylanes of Saki Naka *chawl* wound through a vibrant microcosm of life, weaving its way through a tapestry of thriving businesses. The cramped roads, though barely wide enough for four people to pass but always accommodated six, were brimming with an energy that would make even the grandest boulevards envious. The tantalising aromas of street food wafted through the air, drawing in customers from far and wide.

Sukumar's words echoed in their ears as they made their way through the labyrinthine streets. From sizzling fried samosas to syrup-drenched jalebis, the air was thick with the scent of delectable delights. Mumbai's crowned king, the iconic vada pav, held court alongside various pav-based items, including *missal pav* and *anda pav*. Each bite carried the essence of this vibrant neighbourhood, a symphony of flavours that captured the essence of the underbelly of India.

Amidst the culinary symphony, a whiff of Arabic *ithar*, sold by the Muslim population, danced on the breeze, adding a hint of mystique to the bustling atmosphere. The mingling scents created a sensory tapestry that spoke of the diverse cultural fabric of Saki Naka *chawl*.

As the team moved forward, their senses were momentarily assaulted by a small gutter line on the road ahead, releasing an unpleasant odour. Tytler and Qureshi instinctively covered their noses, their expressions wrinkling in discomfort. However, the local passersby, accustomed to the everyday realities of Saki Naka *chawl*, paid little heed to the stench, focusing instead on navigating the everyday paths and fulfilling their daily tasks.

The team pressed on, blending seamlessly into the crowd, their presence camouflaged amidst the teeming masses. Their eyes remained fixed on the goal that lay ahead: the capture of Aleem, their target. Each step brought them deeper into the heart of this vibrant microcosm, where the line between order and chaos blurred, and the pulse of life thrived in the most unexpected corners.

"You guys are less than 50 metres away from the hotel," Sukumar's urgent messages continued to guide them through the busy streets.

"I think I see it," Ila's voice trembled with a mix of excitement and apprehension.

"Okay, from the hotel, take a left, and you will feel a certain slope. The second building to the left, behind the juice shop, is Aleem's residence in Saki Naka," Sukumar did his best to assist them from a distance.

The narrow roads resembled a twisted maze, where concealed secrets lay buried at every turn, and danger lurked in the shadows. The chaotic surroundings mirrored the rapid beats of their hearts, intensifying the palpable tension in the air.

"Is it a house in pale blue, with stairs on the side?" Yohan verified.

"Exactly," Inspector Siad Kamble, familiar with the *chawl's* layout, confirmed, having sourced the information from his informants from the area.

Despite it not being Aleem's usual hideout, Yohan couldn't help but notice some of his henchmen guarding the entrance to the house. He discreetly signalled to the backup police team, instructing them to position themselves strategically and block as many escape routes as possible. With the armed officers assuming their posts, Yohan crossed the road and approached the henchmen, posing as someone in need of assistance from Aleem. Ila trailed behind, ready to intervene if her boss encountered any trouble.

Approaching the group of henchmen, all clad in black kurtas, Yohan raised his head and asked, "Aleem *bhau hai*?" inquiring about the whereabouts of the notorious goon. The tall, muscular henchman guarding the main entrance remained sceptical of the CBI officer's question, sensing potential trouble. Meanwhile, another henchman slipped inside the house.

A tense standoff ensued as the guard refused to budge, and Yohan, mindful of not escalating the situation in the bustling area filled with commoners, maintained his composure. Suddenly, a loud thud echoed from behind, as if someone had leaped from a considerable height. Seizing the moment, Yohan swiftly struck the entrance guard in the gut, momentarily incapacitating him, and hurled him towards the waiting police officers. Without hesitation, he darted after the source of the noise, igniting a high-speed chase through the entangled alleyways of the *chawl*. The sound of pounding footsteps reverberated, echoing the urgency of the pursuit, as Aleem manoeuvred through the cramped passages. The police gave chase, but their unfamiliarity with the chawl's complex network of turns and sub-gulleys made it challenging to keep up. Aleem's frantic footsteps echoed through the confined spaces, stirring up dust and debris in his wake. As he sprinted past, potted plants were knocked over, their ceramic vessels shattering into pieces. The crashing sound mingled with the cacophony of the chase, adding an eerie undertone to the pursuit. Desperate to elude capture, Aleem's goons trailing behind him unleashed a volley of gunfire, with bullets whizzing through the air.

"Officers. Don't shoot," Yohan screamed even though the chase was intense, ensuring the safety of civilians.

The Mumbai police officers, restrained and experienced, skilfully ducked and weaved, taking cover behind walls and doorways without retaliating. Their focus was solely on capturing Aleem and bringing him to justice without endangering the lives of innocent bystanders.

As the chase reached its climax, Ila, who had been strategically tailing Aleem, seized the opportunity to intervene. Her keen eyes caught a glimpse of an open doorway leading to a courtyard. Calculating her move, she swiftly manoeuvred into position, her agile form blending seamlessly with the shadows. With practised precision, Ila executed a specialised technique she had mastered during her training. As Aleem sprinted towards the courtyard, she sprung into action, gracefully planting her foot in a precise spot. A hidden mechanism, triggered by her well-timed step, caused a metal grate to shoot up from the ground, blocking Aleem's path.

Caught off guard, Aleem stumbled, his momentum abruptly halted. In a split second, Ila closed in, skilfully disarming him and rendering him powerless. The other police officers swiftly converged on the scene, their collective efforts ensuring Aleem was securely restrained.

"She is the best among us all," Yohan said, catching his breath, addressing Aleem, who stood handcuffed with his hands behind his back, surrounded by police officers.

Ila, flushed with exertion and triumph, stepped forward to join Yohan. A hint of a smile played on her lips as she acknowledged the compliment. "We make a good team, Yohan."

Meanwhile, Aleem's face contorted with anger, his complexion turning crimson as he realised he could not elude the relentless pursuit of the police.

"I don't know why you're after me, but this is a grave mistake. You have no idea who I am," Aleem seethed, his fury emanating from his towering frame. His clenched jawline accentuated his intense gaze while beads of sweat traced a path from his long hair down his neck, trickling along his spine. Despite his helplessness, his mind churned with vengeful thoughts, fixated on Ila, the officer who had outwitted him.

****

The room was dark, save for a sliver of light that filtered through the small window. The walls were bare concrete, and the floor was covered in a thin layer of dust. There was a single table in the centre of the room and two chairs on either side. The room was warm and humid, and the air smelled of sweat and fear.

In the corner of the room was a small pot with water on a stool. Next to the pot was a steel glass and a melamine plate. This was where Aleem, the goon, would be kept after the investigation. There was no washroom in the room, so he would have to use a bucket kept in the room. Aleem sat slumped on the floor, his hands bound tightly behind his back. Exhaustion weighed heavily on him, and hunger gnawed at his stomach. He yearned for respite from this gruelling ordeal that stretched endlessly. Hours had turned into an eternity, and he had already endured two rounds of intense questioning.

Sukumar's voice cut through the stifling air, laced with an unsettling calmness, "We could drag this out for days, Aleem. The longer you resist, the harsher it will be. After all, you are accustomed to a much more lavish lifestyle now."

Aleem, his voice strained yet defiant, defended himself, "Rita madam is just a friend. We just met casually."

Yohan spoke up, his confidence unwavering, "High-profile friends can only offer temporary comfort, Aleem, but don't delude yourself into thinking they'll come to your rescue. You're on your own."

"I've survived worse than this. You think you can break me? Think again," Aleem growled, his pyjamas soaked with sweat, the once-prominent kajal running down his face. The intensity in his eyes matched the colour of his neatly trimmed beard. A single earring complimented the profile of his face.

"Loyalty doesn't satisfy hunger, my friend. While your mind may stand the test of time, your body will eventually give in," Sukumar responded, knowing very well a composed demeanour is the best way to deal with a hardened criminal.

"And if you believe your political connections will come to your rescue, you are sorely mistaken. We have no interest in that and have already dismantled any deals involving your connections. We simply need information on Preetam Gowda," Yohan said, his voice steady and controlled.

"I know way too much about too many powerful people. I won't be left here to suffer," Aleem feigned confidence, attempting to assert control over the situation.

"No one is coming for you. Don't underestimate our ability to reach your so-called connections. Just tell us where Preetam Gowda is," Sukumar pressed.

"Who is Preetam Gowda?" Aleem feigned ignorance, a hint of uncertainty creeping into his voice.

Sukumar swiftly threw a set of photographs at him, revealing CCTV footage capturing Aleem and his goons near Preetam's house on the day of his abduction. "We have been tracing the path of your van through multiple surveillance cameras across the city. And once we locate it ourselves, you will be of no use to us. However, the Mumbai police will have a lot of things they would want to investigate regarding numerous pending cases," Yohan strategically played his game like a chess master, each move meticulously calculated.

"Where is that woman who caught me? I just want to warn her about the consequences she will face," Aleem refused to yield easily, attempting to divert their attention.

"Oh, she is the one who is now liaising with your so-called connections to clip your wings. By now, you should know she is quite the formidable player," Yohan taunted, aiming to strike a blow to Aleem's ego.

Aleem's right cheek twitched involuntarily, a sign of his inner struggle to maintain composure in the face of the lead CBI officer's comment. Hunger gnawed at his stomach, exacerbating his frustration and disgust, gradually eroding his mental fortitude. He began scratching his head and beard with an unconventional pace, clearly reflecting his deteriorating state of mind. Yohan keenly observed the goon's diminishing defences, sensing that the opportune moment to strike was drawing near.

"Take a good look at this photo," Yohan raised the picture to Aleem's line of sight. "This woman is Preetam's wife. Every day, she walks to the same police station, hoping they'll find her missing husband. They have a six-year-old daughter who hasn't attended school since her father was abducted."

Aleem fought the urge to look at the photo, just as he had always tried to suppress thoughts about the personal lives of those he kidnapped, threatened, or harmed on behalf of his corporate and influential clients. "I'm tough, sir. This won't break me," he muttered, his voice lacking the conviction he desired.

"I know it won't, Aleem. It's all part of the job, isn't it?" Yohan acknowledged the goon's thoughts, his tone tinged with a hint of understanding. "But imagine if we were to keep you in custody for more than a week with no official record of your arrest."

Aleem listened intently, a growing unease pervading his being as he sensed the conversation veering into unsettling territory.

Suddenly, Sukumar interjected, seamlessly completing his superior's statement as if rehearsed, "Yes, and imagine your wife and three children left to wander the streets with unending tears and disappointment as they search for you."

The weight of Sukumar's words bore down on Aleem, his hardened exterior cracking under the weight of the emotional implications. Deep down, he knew the consequences of his actions had far-reaching ramifications, extending beyond himself. For the first time, doubt flickered in his eyes, hinting at a crack in his armour.

"Why do you police *valas* always have to drag family into everything? Fight like a man. Make it man to man," Aleem scoffed, his male pride on full display.

"Why do you goondas never think about families when harming someone? Be more human," Yohan retorted, matching Aleem's tone.

"As we speak, your wife and children are worrying about you at your house in Kurla. Soon, they will come begging to the police," Sukumar added, his words laden with the weight of a threat.

"And, Aleem, it's not like we're asking you for information on something you did for a leader. Siju is just a businessman. Nothing is going to happen to you," Yohan tried to reassure the goon, emphasising the minimal risk involved for him.

"Sir, in our line of business, betrayal means everything is over," Aleem revealed a glimpse of his vulnerability, his tough exterior cracking under the weight of his past choices.

"In our line of business, a crime means punishment. And as I said, all I want is information on Preetam Gowda, and I will keep you out of this case," Yohan assured, attempting to strike a deal.

"This offer is only valid if you tell us where he is. If we find out on our own, you'll be left empty-handed," Sukumar added, applying pressure. "You should know that based on CCTV tracking, we have already seen your vehicle pass Byculla. There are only so many hideouts you have, Aleem."

"Is he still alive?" Yohan asked, again changing his tone to calm and composed.

Aleem, grappling with a myriad of emotions and the gnawing hunger that plagued him, yearned for this ordeal to be over. Yet, he pondered whether to give in or wait it out, fully aware that the officers might not even need him if their investigation led them directly to the missing man. The mention of 'Byculla' triggered a warning signal in Aleem's mind. He knew that the police were relentlessly pursuing Preetam, and it seemed like a game of cat and mouse with no clear winner thus far.

"Yes, he is alive," Aleem finally revealed, his admission signalling a small victory for the investigators.

Sukumar breathed a sigh of relief, feeling a renewed sense of optimism that they could finally question the missing man and uncover potential leads. "Now tell us, where is he?" Sukumar urged, trying to keep the momentum going, "Come on, Aleem. We have a lot of work to do."

Feeling the doors closing in around him, Aleem let out a heavy sigh, his mind racing as he calculated his options. With a deep breath, he finally revealed the most prized information, "He is at my wife's brother's hideout at Mazgaon."

Slapping both hands on the table, Yohan stood up, knowing that this revelation could lead them to the man who had been missing for weeks and potentially uncover crucial links between Siju and Mekhala's death. "Kamble ji, get your team to raid the location. I want him here as soon as possible. Ila will handle the questioning."

"Sir, please don't arrest my wife or her brother. They have nothing to do with this," Aleem pleaded, visibly upset and desperate to shield his family from harm.

"We'll handle that," Yohan assured, his voice softening for a moment as he recognised the pain in Aleem's eyes, the same pain any person would feel when protecting their loved ones. For a brief moment, he chose to forget that he was standing in front of a criminal.

Yohan left the room to call Ila, updating her on the progress and outlining her next task, while Sukumar focused on completing the necessary formalities with Aleem.

"Ila, we've got Preetam Gowda. Now he's all yours," Yohan said, excitement seeping into his voice.

Ila, who had been outside pursuing a lead after apprehending Aleem, didn't mirror the same level of excitement in her tone.

"Is everything okay, Ila?" Yohan checked, sensing something amiss in her response.

"Yohan, I was tailing those party-organising guys who were at Mekhala's neighbour's house."

"And?"

"It seems like there is a connection between them and the team at the club where Siddharth died."

"What connection?"

"You are right. The fire at the club appears to be a well-planned murder, probably orchestrated to target Siddharth," Ila disclosed.

A surge of conflicting emotions rushed through Yohan's mind. On the one hand, there was a momentary sense of vindication, knowing that his theory about Siddharth's death being more than an accident was indeed correct. On the other hand, this revelation added a new layer of complexity to the case, deepening the mystery surrounding the motives and individuals involved.

Yohan stood there, his phone held tightly in his hand, his mind churning with countless probabilities and potential roadblocks ahead in their pursuit of justice. The realisation that the investigation had just taken another turn fuelled his determination to uncover the truth, no matter the obstacles that stood in their way.

Chapter 13
STILL LEADS RUN DEEP

Siju Ramachandran sat composed in front of the investigators, dressed in a sharp black suit and a crisp white shirt, exuding an air of authority. Beside him sat Rita Khamboj, summoned due to her association with Aleem, the notorious goon involved in Preetam Gowda's abduction. The corporate tycoon and his secretary were engulfed in a cloud of uncertainty as they faced intense questioning from the CBI.

While Yohan was busy following leads regarding the suspicious presence of the party organising team in both locations, his team continued their investigation.

Ila, with her piercing eyes, wasted no time and addressed the duo directly, “Listen carefully. We already have Aleem's confession about kidnapping Preetam. Now we want to know why you killed Mekhala?”

With a touch of impatience, Sukumar added, “Don't play innocent or pretend you don't know her. We are all busy, so let's cut to the chase and get down to business.”

Feeling the mounting pressure, Rita took an aggressive opening stand, retorting, “Are you seriously doubting us based on the words of a criminal?”

“Madam, we have concrete evidence in the form of photographs and call records documenting your meetings.

So, enough with the victim act. It won't work here," Ila didn't flinch.

"Listen, officer. We haven't killed anybody. I'm not convinced these claims will hold in court," Siju mustered his courage and finally spoke up.

"Then why did you kidnap Preetam?" Sukumar asked.

"I haven't instructed anyone to kidnap him," the CEO responded.

"All the circumstantial evidence is against you, Mr. Siju. I suggest you cooperate," Ila pressed.

"You all have nothing against me or Sir," Rita interjected.

"Rita, we have more evidence against you than against your boss," Sukumar shot back.

"There is an obvious link between Preetam's kidnapping and you guys—the news stories and all the media frenzy that followed," Ila added.

"Exactly, Ms. Ila. These are all stories concocted by the media. If anything, we are victims of a vulturous media trial," Siju calmly responded, showing his finesse in skewing narratives to his advantage. Ila observed him silently, knowing that if not guided in the right direction, the business tycoon in front of her could manipulate the situation.

"So you're also claiming that you haven't taken a loan and defaulted?" Ila approached from another angle.

"Is that really under the purview of your investigation? I believe there are more specialised agencies to handle that inquiry," Siju retorted with calculated precision.

Sukumar decided to speak up, defending Ila's expertise, "Sir, you're right, but Ila madam has experience working in the Economic Offences Wing of the CBI, and this falls well within her area of expertise."

Ila appreciated Sukumar's intention to support her credibility, yet she wasn't entirely pleased with his defensive tone.

"In that case, let's discuss that matter. At least these baseless murder claims will no longer be a concern," Siju deflected accusations effortlessly.

"Don't worry, sir. In the murder case, we have enough evidence to request remand, at least for Rita. So you can remain free until then," Sukumar's intentions to rattle Rita were evident.

"Kidnapping, sir. There is no link to the murder, at least according to the previous photographs you flashed," Siju smirked confidently.

"Have you ever spoken to Mekhala, Mr. Siju?" Ila asked

"You must have seen my phone records. So, yes, I did."

"Why?"

"Well, I am an honest man, and my most honest submission, or rather a confession to you, would be that I called her to request that she refrain from publishing the book. It would have a detrimental impact on my business," Siju explained.

"Request or threat?"

"Ila, as the CEO, it is well within my rights to request, or rather, strongly request someone not to exacerbate an issue that would cost my company, our investors, our customers, the children who trust us and our employees. I did what any responsible CEO would do," Siju defended himself with a touch of drama in his presentation.

"So you agree that the book's publication would have significant financial and personal repercussions. That's a solid motive, and it falls well within my purview," Ila responded, not holding back her assertiveness and giving it back in the same tone, having learned a thing or two from Yohan.

"That's plain conjecture," Siju brushed it off, chuckling.

Meanwhile, Sukumar sensed this would be an opportune time to take Rita out of the room. Being in the shadow of her boss, she might feel more confident, and separating her from him could potentially yield more results in their investigation. Rita grumbled and protested as she was escorted to the other room.

Observing her reaction, Siju couldn't help but speak up, his voice laced with defiance, "Do you think separating us will work, Mr. Sukumar? We are neither murderers nor nincompoops. Hang in there, Rita. This will be over soon, as long as you remain composed," Siju's words held a veiled message for Rita, an attempt to caution her against revealing more than necessary.

"Mr. Siju, there is no escaping the Preetam kidnapping case. You have a direct link to it," Ila asserted.

Before responding, Siju waited for the door to close behind Rita. Once it did, he leaned forward and spoke with a calculated tone, "That link will primarily implicate Rita. There is no evidence of me instructing her to do anything."

As Rita left the room, Ila wasn't surprised by the chameleon-like shift in Siju's responses.

"So, betrayal it is, then?"

"No comments. Stupid people who leave trails should be punished."

"Even if they acted on your behalf?"

"I didn't ask anyone to do anything for me. That's merely your speculation."

"Tell me honestly, off the record, do you think Rita should have been more careful?"

"There is nothing off the record in an investigation room, madam. But if you are asking for my general opinion. In that case, she should have been far more intelligent," Siju evaded the question while making it clear that he was displeased with Rita's lack of discretion, allowing trails to be left behind.

"So, you've decided to make her the scapegoat?"

"Ila, I'm not going to entertain baseless speculations. You should know me well enough by now."

"How do you plan to distance yourself from Rita when she is clearly involved in the kidnapping?"

"Read her job description," Siju retorted confidently. "Kidnapping is not part of her responsibilities. I cannot be held accountable for the actions of my employees in their personal capacity."

"Hmmm. Escapist."

"So you are suggesting that Rita will face charges under IPC 363? A possible four-year sentence, then?" Siju smirked, displaying his familiarity with the law.

As Siju continued to exude overconfidence in the room, little did he know that his intelligence was about to be unravelled by a simple trick devised by Ila and Sukumar. Unbeknownst to Siju, Ila had strategically kept her phone connected to Sukumar, allowing Rita to eavesdrop on every word spoken in the other room.

A mixture of anger and shock washed over Rita as she listened to Siju's conversation. "That bastard," she muttered under her breath, unable to contain her frustration.

Seizing the moment, Sukumar saw an opportunity to leverage Rita's vulnerability. "So, Rita, your only way out is to become a cooperating witness. Otherwise, it's clear that your boss is abandoning you."

"He thinks I'm stupid? I'll show him who's truly foolish," Rita responded.

As the intensity of the interrogation grew, both Ila and Sukumar's attention was abruptly diverted by the persistent ringing of their phones. It was highly unusual for Yohan to interrupt them during an interrogation. However, sensing the potential urgency, they quickly picked up the calls.

"*Anna*, Ila, pack your bags immediately. We need to leave for Assam as soon as possible."

"But, Yohan, what about Siju and Rita? What should we do with them?" Ila questioned.

"They are important links, but for now, let Kamble and the team take over their questioning."

"Boss, what's going on? What's happening in Assam?" Sukumar interjected.

"The truth we've been seeking, the answers we've been chasing—they're waiting for us in Assam," Yohan declared.

*****

As the team embarked on the journey from Guwahati Airport to the city where the CBI guest house awaited them, they finally had a moment to catch up with Yohan. The flight had provided them with a much-needed opportunity to rest and regain their energy. The road stretched ahead, mostly two-lane highways flanked by lush greenery. Occasionally, they passed clusters of houses and commercial establishments, giving the surroundings a quaint, small-town charm devoid of the bustling traffic and noise of metropolitan cities.

Still groggy from lack of sleep, Sukumar found himself dozing off in the backseat of the car, his snores echoing through the vehicle. Although the sound was rather loud, Ila and Yohan refrained from waking him. They empathised with his fatigue, knowing the intense weeks they had all endured. However, Ila couldn't help but feel a sense of anticipation, eager for an update from Yohan regarding his discoveries and their plan of action in the upcoming city.

"Yohan, we couldn't update you about Siju's interrogation or discuss what you found out. Why did we leave everything and come to Assam?" Ila inquired, eager to understand the purpose of their trip.

"Well, Ila, the *modus operandi* of both fires and your findings about the party organising companies being the same intrigued me."

"What did you discover?"

"Take a look at these photos," Yohan handed over the screenshots of a man wearing a sideways cap, an oversized black t-shirt, and cargo pants. The photos were taken from an influencer's Instagram reel, captured at the club where Siddharth died in the fire. The man in the photos had distinct Mongoloid facial features.

"Who is he?" Ila questioned, studying the photos intently.

"*Thamba*, Ila. I have more photos for you," Yohan showed Ila another picture, taken outside Mekhala's building. Among a group of people in catering uniforms, one man's face was circled in red ink. Although he wore a mask, certain facial features were visible.

"Even with the mask on, you can see the similarities in the eyes, right?" Yohan pointed out.

Ila quickly analysed the eyelids and forehead, comparing the two photos. Yes, the epicanthic fold, monolid eyes, and absence of a hair-ledge point on the forehead. It's almost certainly the same person."

"Good catch, Ila."

"But tell me one thing, Yohan. Why does this connection bring us to Assam?" Ila sought further clarity on their location choice.

"It's a good question, but not the right question, Ila," Yohan replied, waiting for Ila to understand the bigger picture.

Sukumar, who had just woken up from his slumber, peered through half-opened eyes at the blurry images of

Yohan, Ila, and their driver. "Ila madam, the question he's looking for is, who is this man?" he chimed in.

Yohan's smile widened, recognising Sukumar's instinct to seize every opportunity to show off his instincts. It was a testament to their years of partnership, where Sukumar could understand his boss's intentions.

"*Anna*, right on cue," Yohan remarked, giving Sukumar a forearm salute before turning his attention back to Ila. "And that is the right question."

"So, who is he, boss?" Ila asked eagerly.

Yohan reached into his bag and handed Ila a file. As she opened it, her eyes scanned the details, including the name Banjur Basamatary, accompanied by an old photograph. Ila's face lit up with recognition, realising the significance of their presence in Assam.

"Is he our guy?" Ila asked, still trying to grasp the reality of the complex situation they found themselves in.

"Absolutely, the very same Banjur Basamatary, one of Anup Baruah's close aides," Yohan confirmed, revealing the direct connection of their mysterious man to Anup Baruah, the leader of the Assam Tiger Liberation Force.

Banjur Basumatary was a man well-known within the circles of the Assam Tiger Liberation Force (ATLF) and individuals who closely monitored their activities. He had gained a reputation for orchestrating various events, including acts of violence, on behalf of the organisation and its leader, Anup Baruah. However, while his files did not directly indicate his involvement in killing people, his actions indirectly led to the deaths of several individuals. The fact that Banjur Basumatary was present at both the crime scenes involving Mekhala and Siddharth caught Yohan's attention, drawing parallels between the cases and the activities of the ATLF. Yohan understood that Banjur's role went beyond being a mere participant in the organisation's activities. His involvement in the fire at Mekhala's event and the tragic fire incident involving Siddharth hinted at a sinister motive that extended beyond random acts of violence. Yohan couldn't help but wonder if Banjur's role in these incidents was part of a larger plan, with implications far beyond what they had initially anticipated.

"And where are we going to get this man, Yohan?"

"Ila, our intelligence team has received solid information that he has fled to Assam, specifically Tinsukia. It's one of the few areas where the ATLF has a significant presence," Yohan revealed.

Sukumar's concern was evident as he interjected, "It's not going to be easy to get Banjur from the ATLF den, Yohan. It is a highly dangerous area."

"I understand, *anna.* But this is all part of the job description," Yohan replied, a confident smile gracing his face.

"Catching murderers, yes. Getting killed in the process, no," Sukumar's tone grew more serious as he voiced his worries

On the other hand, Ila was eager for another shot at taking down a criminal, fuelled by the adrenaline rush from the recent Saki Naka episode in Mumbai.

"*Anna*, don't worry. I'll take the bullet that has your name written on it. But we are going to Tinsukia," Yohan remained unshaken.

⁂

Tinsukia, the northernmost district of Upper Assam, is a complex blend of history, tradition, industrial activity, and coal mining. Despite these complexities, the area was often engulfed in a sea of turbulence. The infamous ATLF had established one of its bases here, and their growing influence was seen as both an occasional blessing and, more often, a curse by the locals. The reserve forest areas of Upper Dehing and Kahatangpani, enveloped in dense greenery, offered a stunning view. However, beneath the shadow of this beauty and its inaccessibility, the ATLF found the perfect stronghold, impervious to regular police forces. Their expanding presence and the awareness of the potential havoc they could wreak meant that the government hesitated to deploy its elite forces, not out of fear, but due to concerns over the negative impact on the civilians living nearby. Although the area still fell under Indian sovereignty, the ATLF's activities made life challenging for law enforcement. For the common person, the vast wilderness of the reserve forest represented untamed beauty, wildlife, and the sounds of rustling leaves and bird calls, yet the danger lurking within was a constant threat.

It was into these untamed terrains that the CBI team, led by Yohan and accompanied by the local police force, ventured to assess the area concealing their most crucial lead or suspect, who was crucial for this investigation to proceed. They navigated the narrow and winding Digboi-Pengaree Bordumsa road, moving through thick vegetation that created a tunnel-like ambiance with trees intertwining overhead, forming a natural archway.

Suddenly, the car screeched to a halt, causing the vehicle behind to brake abruptly. Sensing something amiss, Yohan stepped out of his car and approached the police jeep, escorting them on the desolate and eerie road. The silence was broken only by the sound of rustling leaves and the distant chirping of birds.

"Pushkar ji, why have we stopped?" Yohan inquired, his eyes scanning the surroundings.

Pushkar, the CI (Circle Inspector), looked visibly petrified as he spoke, "Sir, you see those tent-like structures over there?" He pointed towards a cluster of structures amidst the dense foliage.

Yohan raised an eyebrow and gestured for Pushkar to continue.

"That is the makeshift base of the ATLF, sir," Pushkar explained, his voice trembling. "They will have hundreds of their militants guarding every entry. We need more forces, sir."

Yohan observed the fear etched on Pushkar's face and the unease permeating the rest of the team. He remained calm, his eyes still fixed on the hidden base.

Concealed under the thick foliage, a makeshift shelter emerged, serving as the secret base of the Assam Tiger Liberation Front. In this covert sanctuary, the time seemed suspended, as nature's whispers blended with hushed conversations and the crackling of a modest campfire, casting an air of suspense and intrigue. The shelter, fashioned from natural materials, seamlessly blended with its surroundings. Camouflage netting drapes over branches, disguising its presence, while fallen leaves and twigs create a natural floor. The forest's sounds, amplified by the absence of urban noise, served as a constant reminder of their deep connection to the untamed wilderness.

As Yohan surveyed the scene, his gaze shifted to the well-organised arrangement of the tents and the vigilant sentries strategically positioned around the perimeter. The make-shift swings and barrels served as seating, providing a semblance of comfort in their rugged environment. The ATLF militants had transformed this secluded spot into their sanctuary, a place where they planned and executed their operations. The distant figures of armed militants patrolling the perimeter caught Yohan's attention. Their vigilance was evident, as they moved with a sense of purpose, their eyes scanning for any signs of intruders. It was clear that the ATLF took their security seriously, leaving no room for complacency.

Yohan handed the binoculars to Ila and Sukumar, allowing them to witness the scene for themselves. The seriousness of the situation weighed heavily upon them as they realised the magnitude of the task at hand. The ATLF stronghold presented a formidable challenge, and their operation to apprehend Banjur Basumatary would require meticulous planning, precision, and support from additional forces. The hushed conversations and faint noises emanating from the base served as a constant reminder of the imminent danger.

"Come on, guys, let's get going!" Yohan urged.

His face etched with confusion and fear, Pushkar hesitated at Yohan's words. Sukumar, too, couldn't fathom his boss's rationale, his brows furrowed in scepticism.

"Sir, we can't go there with just a few people. There are hundreds of them guarding the fort," Puskhar voiced his apprehensions.

"I understand your concerns, Pushkar. But I just want to assess the entry points to the top. What if we need to raid their hideout sometime?" Yohan locked eyes with Sukumar even though he addressed Pushkar, fed up with the latter's push back .

Sukumar rolled his eyes, a mix of exasperation and worry evident on his face. Reluctantly, he climbed back into the car, joining the rest of the team. The engine purred to life, but the speed was deliberately kept slow to avoid drawing unwanted attention.

As the convoy advanced along the treacherous path, tension hung like a palpable entity. Suddenly, a deafening thud reverberated through the surroundings, jolting everyone inside the vehicles. The lead jeep lost control, teetering dangerously close to the edge of the narrow road. The driver's swift reflexes allowed them to apply the brakes, preventing a disastrous plunge down the cliff below.

In the chaos that ensued, the officers scrambled out of their vehicles, their hearts pounding with adrenaline. Sensing the gravity of the situation, Yohan and his team swiftly followed suit. Pushkar rushed towards them, a sense of urgency gripping his every word.

"Sir, let's leave. This is a deliberate act by the militants to create a diversion and notify them if anyone is nearing their turf," Pushkar's words resonated with an amplified sense of urgency.

Suddenly, a group of men clad in light green khaki shirts and pants emerged from behind the dense forest, catching Yohan, Sukumar, Ila, Pushkar and the rest of the officers off guard. The men swiftly encircled the police and CBI team, forming a barrier that trapped them in the midst of a tense standoff. Their attire, meticulously chosen for camouflage, blended seamlessly with the surrounding foliage. The khaki fabric bore traces of wear, suggesting their experience in the field. Black cloth masks concealed their identities, adding an air of mystery and intimidation. Each militant wielded a formidable array of weapons, ranging from the lethal AK-103 and AK-63 assault rifles to the reliable Type 56 rifles. The CBI team, unarmed, could only rely on their training and wits while the police officials instinctively raised their basic pistols in defence.

Without warning, the militants launched a coordinated attack, striking the police officers from behind as they circled the CBI team. The vicious assault sent shockwaves through the tense atmosphere, escalating the danger to a new level. Yohan's instincts kicked in, recognising the urgent need for escape and regrouping. He gestured to Pushkar, conveying a silent message to seek refuge in the safety of their vehicle.

Amidst the chaos, a figure emerged from the militants' ranks, exuding an air of authority. Positioned between two heavily armed individuals acting as his bodyguards, he approached the trapped team with a chilling blend of authority and hostility. "Why are you here? This is our territory," the leader, Neigham demanded, his voice laced with a stern warning.

Yohan's mind raced as he assessed the tense situation. He knew that aggression wouldn't work in their favour at this moment. With a calm demeanour, he stepped forward, his hands casually folded behind his head, a gesture meant to convey non-threatening intentions.

"This is just a routine visit to ensure everything is alright," Yohan stated firmly, his voice projecting a sense of authority.

However, Neigham, remained unconvinced, his eyes narrowed in suspicion. "Nobody comes here without a reason, mister," he retorted, his voice tinged with hostility.

Undeterred, Yohan continued to speak, his words carefully chosen. With subtle finger signals from his hands at the back, barely noticeable to the others, he communicated to Pushkar, urging him to return to the car slowly. Time was of the essence, and Yohan needed to buy as much of it as possible.

"Don't believe me? Pushkar, please show them the files kept in the front seat," Yohan instructed, his tone confident. He hoped that Pushkar would notice his phone on the seat, which Yohan had previously instructed Pushkar to use and dial a certain number in case of trouble. Yohan had made prior arrangements, knowing the risks of their mission, ensuring that backup forces were on standby, ready to come to their aid in the event of an attack.

Yohan's eyes flickered with determination and hope as he continued his conversation with the militants. Time seemed to slow down, every passing second intensifying the underlying tension. Finally, the moment arrived. Yohan's face lit up as he saw Pushkar manoeuvring with the phone.

"Why are you attacking the policemen?" Ila boldly questioned Neigham, her voice steady despite the dangerous situation.

"Do you have a problem?" The leader sneered, grabbing his rifle and placing it on Ila's shoulder. Slowly, he moved it down her arm, the cold metal pressing against her skin and drawing a small trickle of blood.

"We told you this is a routine visit. You are unnecessarily inviting trouble," Ila responded, her eyes darting towards Yohan and Pushkar, silently urging them to use this distraction to their advantage.

Yohan rolled his eyes at Ila, signalling her to stay calm and keep the conversation going. He knew that escalating the situation further could jeopardise their chances of escape.

"Trouble? And you think you can put me in trouble?" The leader's smirk revealed his patriarchal mindset, demeaning Ila for being a woman.

"I am more than enough for you," Ila said, her smile tinged with tension as she tried to keep the conversation going. Neigham called out to his men, instructing them to halt their movements. He set his rifle aside and stepped closer to Ila, a challenging glint in his eyes.

"Come on then, show me what you've got," he taunted, inviting her to engage in a physical duel. Ila, determined and prepared, lowered her hands, ready to defend herself.

Yohan, taken aback by Ila's deviation from the planned course of action, quickly moved forward and positioned himself between Neigham and Ila. "We don't need trouble, people," he urged, trying to diffuse the escalating tension.

Neigham's eyes lingered on Ila's face, his eyes filled with an unsettling mix of lust and aggression. He edged closer, the distance between them shrinking, until he was but a breath away from her face, their eyes locked in an unspoken conversation. The sweat dripping down from her forehead seemed to add a radiant allure to her face, captivating his attention. Ila, no stranger to the objectifying stares of men, could sense the predatory desire in his eyes. It was a look she had encountered countless times before, a demeaning gaze that devalued her worth as a woman.

Suddenly, from a distance, the piercing wails of sirens echoed through the air, heralding the arrival of salvation in the form of three jeeps and a bus brimming with reinforcements. The blaring sirens served as a warning to the militants and their leader, urging them to hasten their plans and seek refuge in hidden corners. Sensing the imminent danger, Neigham forcefully shoved Ila aside, his voice echoing with urgency as he ordered his troops to retreat.

But Ila, undeterred and encouraged by the approaching reinforcements, swiftly gathered her resolve and surged forward, determined to capture the leader as his threats had provoked her enough to do so. Confidence radiated from her every move as she closed in on her target. However, the tall and robust man, fuelled by desperation, struck with lightning speed, delivering a devastating blow with his elbow that crashed into Ila's face, shattering her nose and causing crimson streams of blood to gush forth. Despite the pain and the red haze clouding her vision, Ila's determination remained unyielding as she clung tenaciously to Neigham, refusing to release her grip.

With each passing moment, the militant leader unleashed a barrage of fierce punches, each strike intended to break her spirit. But Ila, fuelled by her unwavering resolve, weathered the storm, her body bruised and battered, but her grip unrelenting. Meanwhile, Yohan, with fire in his eyes, pursued the remaining militants who were still locked in combat with the police. However, witnessing Ila enduring a barrage of blows, he knew he couldn't leave her defenceless. In a burst of adrenaline, he swiftly changed course and rushed back to her aid.

As the jeeps closed in, causing panic to grip the fleeing militants, Neigham and Ila's ego forced them to lock themselves in a fierce duel that seemed too unnecessary for both parties involved. Suddenly, a thunderous gunshot pierced the air, jolting everyone on the battleground. The deafening sound reverberated through their bodies, momentarily paralysing them in shock. In that split second of distraction, Ila's grip loosened, and the leader seized the opportunity to break free, darting away to escape into the chaos.

Yohan's heart pounded in his chest as he raced forward, his eyes fixated on the blood trickling from the wounds. Determination etched upon his face, he knew every second mattered. Amid the pandemonium, Sukumar stood motionless, clutching his abdomen with a white-knuckled grip. The agony etched on his face revealed the gravity of his sacrifice. He had taken a bullet meant for Ila, attempting to shield her from harm. Sukumar's body crumpled to the ground, his knees colliding with the earth first, followed by the rest of his being, blood pooling around him.

"*Anna*! *Anna*!" Yohan's voice cracked with anguish and disbelief as he rushed to Sukumar's side. Ila sat on the ground, her face frozen in shock, her eyes fixed on Sukumar, who fought to cling to consciousness.

"I told you it was dangerous. Bu... but don't worry," Sukumar's words faltered as he struggled to speak through the searing pain. "You are going to catch those bas... bastards," his voice trailed off, weakened by his injuries.

Chapter 14
MALICE MAKETH A MENACING MILITANT

"What the hell is happening, Verma?" The Home Minister's voice reverberated through his office, filled with anger and frustration. Director Jagat Verma sat across from the Minister, maintaining a calm demeanour as he listened to the furious leader vent his rage.

"You know that the ATLF issue is a very sensitive one, and how dare your officer enter their territory without prior permission? What kind of circus are you running there?" The Minister's voice boomed, his words laced with indignation.

Yohan, connected via video conferencing, sat with his head bowed, barely registering the conversation. Flashes of Sukumar lying in a pool of blood on the ground replayed relentlessly in his mind. The weight of responsibility pressed heavily on Yohan's shoulders, knowing that he had ignored Sukumar's warnings about the danger.

"Sir, they had strong evidence to pursue the lead," Verma defended his team, determined to stand his ground despite the precarious situation.

"Even if they did, you were supposed to keep me in the loop. This is not the first time. Even with Kailash *ji,* your officers acted on impulse. And now we have one officer fighting for his life in the hospital," the Minister retorted, his voice filled with disappointment and anger.

"Sir, I take full responsibility. The timing was crucial for them to apprehend the culprit," Verma reasoned.

"Even so, you cannot deal with a matter concerning internal security without obtaining approval from the Home Ministry," the Minister declared firmly.

"I am sorry, but the team is very close to solving it."

"Verma, are you telling me that your team will be able to infiltrate the ATLF territory and apprehend the suspect?" the Home Minister's Secretary interjected, his voice tinged with scepticism.

Yohan, who had remained quiet until now, rose from his chair in the hospital waiting room and spoke with a hint of defiance. "It is not the bloody ATLF's territory, sir. It is the Union of India's territory," he declared firmly, his words resonating with a sense of National pride. The room fell silent for a moment, but soon, a surge of pride filled the hearts of those present.

"Yohan, calm down," Verma instructed, trying to diffuse the tension.

"He is not in a state to attend this meeting. Yohan, we will discuss the rest with your superior," the Secretary declared, abruptly ending the video call. "Verma *ji*, this is unacceptable. Your officer has crossed his limits."

"Parikh *ji*, please understand his situation. His teammate is fighting for his life," Verma tried to reason with the Secretary.

The Home Minister rose from his seat, his expression grave, and walked toward the large map of the country displayed on the wall. "Parikh is right, Verma. I am pulling your team off this case. We will assign the ATF to apprehend this Banjur character, and a team from RAW will handle further investigation."

"No, sir. You can't do that," Verma exclaimed, his frustration reaching boiling point. He slammed his hands on the table, momentarily forgetting the authority he was addressing.

"Excuse me?" The Minister's tone conveyed surprise and mild offence.

"Parikh *Ji*, could you give us a moment?" Verma requested.

The Home Minister nodded and his aide obediently left the room, closing the door behind him. The air grew heavy with tension as Verma and the Minister faced each other, both aware of the weight of the decisions made at that crucial moment.

"Verma, I understand the situation your officer is in, and that's precisely why I believe it's best to assign a team more adept at combat to handle this."

"No, sir, you don't understand," Verma retorted, his voice tinged with urgency. "My team has given their all. They are on the brink of cracking this case. Pulling them out now would not only demoralise the entire CBI but also jeopardise the progress we have made."

"I can't take that risk, Verma. Please understand this; it's nothing personal. This is strictly a professional decision."

"No, sir, it's not just professional anymore. It's personal," Verma declared passionately. "I have one of my most brilliant officers, who is not even a field agent, lying in the hospital after taking a bullet to save his teammate. I have two other officers willing to go to any lengths to solve this case. I am not asking for a favour, sir. I am just saying that this is personal for us. And if we don't crack this, I will resign from my post and take full responsibility in front of the media and the public for any consequences which follow."

Verma stood his ground, unwavering in his support for his team. He had immense belief in Yohan and the others, and he knew that standing up for them, even if it meant sacrificing his career, was the right thing to do. While some bosses stole credit, Verma willingly took all the responsibility and agreed to be the fall guy if needed.

"Verma, don't think I'm some terrible villain trying to bring you all down," the Minister spoke with a softer tone, his anger subsiding. "Both you and I want justice to prevail. But remember, you have one week. After that, the case will be handed over to RAW."

"Thank you, sir, and I apologise for raising my voice."

"It's understandable in your line of business, Verma. Jai Hind," the Minister concluded.

Verma reciprocated with a resounding 'Jai Hind' before leaving the room, a sense of victory coursing through his veins. He hurriedly dialled Yohan's number, eager to update him on the situation.

"Yohan, how is Sukumar doing?"

"He's still not out of danger."

"And how are you holding up, son?"

"I've been better. It's just that he warned me," Yohan replied, his voice trembling with emotion.

Verma could sense Yohan's pain and wanted to be there for his protégé.

"Is Ila with you?"

"No, sir. But no matter what, the show must go on. I sent her to strategise our next move with the local police."

"Oh, okay."

"Sir, what did the Home Minister say?"

"Don't bother too much about that. I have handled it," Verma assured him, not wanting Yohan to carry the burden of the conversation.

"I'm sorry, sir, you had to go through this because of me."

"Don't worry, Yohan. I'll manage as much as I can. But we need results soon."

"I won't let you down, sir."

"Yeah, he has given us one week. If not, he will hand over the case to RAW," Verma informed Yohan about the Minister's ultimatum.

"He won't do that, sir," Yohan's voice suddenly took on his trademark cockiness. "He would have done it long ago if he wanted to."

Verma decided it wasn't the right time to disclose the details of his conversation with the Minister. He changed the subject instead.

"Also, I am sending a new member to the team."

"Why, sir?" Yohan couldn't fathom the thought of replacing his dear colleague, who was more than just a teammate to him.

"Listen to me, Yohan. Now is not the time to debate. The officer's name is Gunang Gogoi. She is from Assam and well-versed in ATLF politics."

Yohan didn't know much about the new officer but had learned to trust Verma implicitly. He understood that Verma's decisions were always made with their best interests at heart.

There was a tap on Yohan's shoulder, and he quickly turned around. Without realising that Verma was still on the call, he exclaimed, "Shweta!"

"Who is there?"

Yohan stood there, caught off guard, not knowing how to respond. Shweta remained silent, a slight blush colouring her cheeks as she saw Yohan's face light up with delight at seeing her.

"It's a journalist, sir."

"Oh, the same Bihar Ashraf case journalist. Nice, my boy."

Yohan was surprised, “How do you know, sir?”

“You think you're the only one who gets updates from Sukumar?” Verma chuckled.

“Typical *anna*. Can’t keep anything to himself.”

The thought of Sukumar's humour and dedication brought a smile and a renewed sense of determination to both Verma and Yohan.

“You carry on. And, son, I know the deadline is tight, but relax if you can,” Verma said before hanging up the call.

Yohan had always appreciated Verma's concern for him and knew he was fortunate to have him as a mentor.

“How come you're here, Shweta?” Yohan asked, genuinely curious.

“Apparently, that's what girlfriends do when their lover is disturbed,” Shweta replied with a playful smile.

“Girlfriend? Isn't that a bit too cheesy, Shweta?” Yohan teased.

“Relax, Yohan. Don't get all uncomfortable.”

“No, it's not that. I genuinely appreciate you being here… I really do,” Yohan reassured her.

“Oh, there's a 'but,' really?” Shweta raised an eyebrow.

“It's not like that. You are an amazing ‘girlfriend’,” Yohan said, using air quotes, “But you're an even better journalist.”

“Yeah, and that too, a CBI officer's girlfriend,” Shweta replied with a smirk.

“So this can't just be a visit to meet me.”

“Of course not. I'm resourceful, as you know, Mr. CBI Officer.” Shweta pulled out some documents from her bag and handed them to Yohan, who quickly scanned the papers.

Shweta pointed to the date on one of the documents and explained, “See, this is from 2009, an excerpt of Adinarayan's interview with Anup Baruah. He was the only journalist to have ever secured an interview with the ATLF leader.”

"Why bring this to me now, Shweta?"

"Because Adinarayan is also in Assam now. Remember, he leaked the news to me about you guys investigating the Delhi-based employee," Shweta revealed.

"What?" Yohan shouted. He hadn't forgotten that Adinarayan had somehow obtained information about their investigation into Zulekha early on but hadn't revealed her name to Shweta. Since then, Yohan had been harbouring suspicions about Adinarayan, waiting for more evidence before confronting him. Shweta's additional tip about Adinarayan's presence in Assam raced through Yohan's mind, triggering a cascade of questions. The two main ones that surfaced were: What could be Adinarayan's motive for killing his wife? And what connection to Anup Baruah had brought him to Assam now?

Without wasting any time, he dialled Ila's number, knowing she was the best person for the task.

"Yes, boss. We are planning the operation to apprehend Banjur," Ila apprised immediately upon receiving the call.

"I'll take care of that, Ila. I have another assignment for you."

"What is it, boss?"

"Adinarayan is in Assam. I need you to capture him and question him thoroughly. Find out his connection to the ATLF. Most importantly, I want to know who provided him with the intel on Zulekha's investigation," Yohan explained, emphasising the importance of the task.

"On it, Yohan."

***

Gunang Gogoi, the young and determined officer in her late twenties, stood before her new boss, Yohan, confidently introducing herself. "Hello, sir. I am Gunang Gogoi."

Yohan gave her a rushed nod, "Welcome to the team, Gunang. Unfortunately, we have no time for a proper orientation. We need to jump right into the case."

Gunang maintained her composure, ready to take on the challenges ahead. "Of course, sir. I'm prepared to contribute in any way I can."

Yohan turned to Pushkar. "Right now, we are strategising our operation to enter the ATLF territory in Upper Dehing, capture Banjur Basumatary and take him into our custody. Tell us your plan of action, Pushkar?"

Pushkar turned on the presentation screen to display his plan. "Sir, first, we will send drones to scan the location from the top. This will help us gather crucial location intelligence and plan the attack more effectively. Once we have a clear understanding of the area, we'll enter through the entry points we have captured on camera."

Yohan examined the plan, considering the potential risks. After a moment of contemplation, he voiced his concerns. "I don't think that is a good idea. The drones will alert them, and it will sabotage the operation."

Pushkar, eager to defend their proposed approach persisted, "But, sir... how do we enter without knowing their location?"

Gunang, sensing an opportunity to contribute, stepped forward. Yohan's curiosity was piqued, as he knew she was from Assam and had firsthand knowledge of the dangers posed by the ATLF.

"Can I suggest something, sir?"

"Go ahead, Gunang. What do you have in mind?"

"Sir, this is a temporary base for the ATLF," Gunang started, her voice filled with purpose. "They avoid cooking any food on-site, fearing that the fire and smell might attract unwanted attention."

Yohan, intrigued by Gunang's initial statement, nodded approvingly. “Mmm, hmm. I'm listening. Go on.”

“Typically, they would seek assistance from locals who sympathise with their cause or use various techniques like blackmail,” Gunang continued. “In some cases, these militants even marry members of the local community, and their families send food to the base through their children to avoid creating suspicion.”

“And, of course, neither our army nor our police would ever harm any child. So, what do you suggest we do, Gunang?” Yohan asked.

Gunang pondered for a moment before responding, “What if we intercept the carriers who deliver the food and discreetly follow them? This way, we might be able to trace the route back to the base.”

Pushkar, unable to contain his concern, interrupted with a valid point, “But, Gunang madam, that could be risky. The carriers would notice any significant activity or movement towards them.”

“That’s a fair point,” Gunang nodded.

“What if we spike their food, incapacitate them, and then launch our attack?” an enthusiastic Pushkar suggested.

Hearing both sides, Yohan stepped in, providing a realistic perspective. “I'm not sure that will work, Pushkar. These militants are well-trained and likely have protocols in place even for their meals. They might have a select few individuals who sample the food first to assess any potential risks before the rest consume it.”

Gunang affirmed Yohan's observation, “Yes, sir, I've heard of similar protocols.”

Pushkar's impatience grew, and he voiced his frustration, “Then what do we do?”

Yohan got up from his seat, walked forward and began mapping his strategy on the board. “Gunang's idea about using the food channel is valid, and Pushkar, your concerns about visible activity uphill are also valid. Going directly to their terrain isn't a smart strategy. We need to find a way to entice them to come downhill."

"But how do we get them to come downhill?" Gunang asked.

Yohan's eyes gleamed with passion as he turned to his team, "Have you heard of the Fabian strategy?"

"Vaguely, yes, sir," Gunang responded. Pushkar, on the other hand, furrowed his brow, racking his brain to recall the details.

A smile tugged at the corners of Yohan's lips. He had a natural inclination for teaching, and whenever the opportunity arose, he couldn't resist sharing his knowledge. Deep within him, a hidden professor was waiting to impart wisdom. He quickly gave them a refresher course.

In the realm of military strategy, the Fabian strategy takes its name from Quintus Fabius Maximus Verrucosus, a Roman general of ancient times. It embodies a cautious approach, steering clear of confrontation with a formidable adversary. Instead, it embraces a war of attrition and guerrilla warfare, slowly eroding the enemy's strength.

In this cunning survival strategy, the focus shifts away from direct confrontations to a strategy of defence and surprise attacks. The weaker side keeps the conflict alive through swift, unexpected strikes, gradually wearing down the enemy's strength and morale. They rely on guerrilla tactics, launching ambushes and raids to cut off supplies and weaken the enemy's resolve. This approach allows them to gather their strength and solidify their stance when the fighting momentarily eases. And when the odds turn insurmountable, retreating tactically isn't a sign of defeat but a smart decision to save their forces for a better chance at victory.

Pushkar, still trying to grasp the full extent of the strategy, asked, "So what do we do exactly, sir?"

Yohan smiled, his mind brimming with the plan. "First, we cut off their food supply. Once at least two meals don't arrive, they will send some people to check. We will intercept and detain those individuals. This will prompt the ATLF to send reinforcements to the village. We will station some of our team members there to neutralise them. Meanwhile, the majority of our force will be positioned near the entry points of the uphill route. We'll deploy bombs at their base, forcing them to come down, where we'll be ready to launch an attack and apprehend them. Remember, these will be hungry and tired individuals, making our task slightly easier."

"I will send my team to trace the food supply network now itself," Pushkar announced, his sense of urgency evident as he rose from his seat, hurrying to get things in motion.

"Meanwhile, Gunang, I have another task for you," Yohan said, his attention shifting towards his new team member. Gunang stood at attention, a hint of disappointment crossing her face. She had hoped to be part of the ATLF strategic attack mission, but being a newcomer, she understood the importance of following the boss's decision.

"What is it, sir?" Gunang asked.

"Before Zulekha joined Brighter, she worked as a journalist in Dibrugarh. I want you to gather more information about her previous investigations and uncover anything she may have discovered," Yohan instructed.

"Okay, sir."

"Pushkar, while you trace the network, I will prepare the troops for our attack on the camp. We are on a tight deadline, so there's no room for mistakes or setbacks," Yohan declared, standing tall with his hands resting on his waist as he surveyed the board, filled with images and plans.

Just as the intensity in the room grew, Yohan's phone buzzed on the table behind him. He quickly picked it up, seeing Ila's name on the screen. "Give me some good news, Ila."

"I got him, Yohan. I got Adinarayan."

"Brilliant stuff, Ila."

"And there is something you must know. It is really shocking."

Yohan and Ila engaged in a conversation, exchanging crucial information. With each passing moment, Yohan's expression shifted from elation to cautious optimism.

"Take him to Delhi, Ila. We will hopefully join you after capturing Banjur."

"Good luck with that, boss."

"Oh, and Ila, I want you to look into something else as well. If we can establish that connection, we'll be very close to cracking this case."

*****

Chapter 15

ALL IS FAIR IN GOOD INTENTIONS AND WAR

The narrow road connecting the hill to the village in Upper Dehing was shrouded in eerie silence as the late evening darkness descended. On this treacherous path, a scene of imminent conflict was about to unfold. The police force, led by a resolute Yohan, stood prepared for the long-awaited confrontation with the militants. The air was heavy with tension, the anticipation palpable.

The police team, armed mostly with INSAS rifles and 7.62 FAL, and the fuel of resolve in their eyes, took their positions strategically along the road. Yohan, his grip firm on his gun, surveyed the surroundings, his heart pounding in his chest. This was the moment they had all been waiting for—to capture Banjur Basumatary, the elusive criminal and close aide to the absconding ATLF leader, Anup Baruah. More than anything, he believed Banjur could fill the missing pieces, especially owing to his mysterious presence in the deaths of Mekhala and Siddharth.

In the militants' camp, more than 24 hours had passed since any semblance of food had reached their starving bellies. The absence of their fellow soldiers, who had ventured into the village to investigate the disrupted supply, only added to the growing sense of unease. Banjur, weakened by hunger, lay on the makeshift bunk, his eyes betraying his desperation. The camp leader, Neigham, approached him with a tinge of remorse etched on his face towards his prized guest whose protection was entrusted to him. "I am sorry, sir. This has never happened before," Neigham said.

Banjur, his stomach rumbling, looked up at Neigham. His hunger-induced frustration was evident in his voice, "Are the people who went looking for our supplies back yet?"

"No, I have sent some more people to find them," Neigham replied. "By the way, did you speak to Commander Anup *da*?"

"Not today, Neigham. I spoke to him when I was in Mumbai," Banjur confirmed. "Hey, how long has it been since you sent the second set of people?"

"About two hours ago."

"This seems like a tra…" Before Banjur could voice his concerns about the situation, a thunderous explosion shattered the stillness. The deafening explosion ripped through the camp, engulfing the surroundings in a blaze of fury. Flames danced hungrily, devouring everything in their path. Panic etched itself onto the faces of Neigham and Banjur as they witnessed the horrifying sight of two militants being torn into shreds by the onslaught of the bombs. The shock of the unexpected assault paralysed them for a moment, their eyes widening in disbelief. As chaos ensued in the camp, the militants scrambled desperately to salvage what they could from the wreckage. The crackling fire cast eerie shadows, amplifying the sense of urgency and fear that permeated the air. With smoke billowing around them, they grabbed their weapons, ammunition, and any supplies within reach. Their movements were frenzied, driven by a primal instinct to survive.

Amidst the swirling chaos, the militants made their decision. Realising the precariousness of their situation, they made a split-second choice to abandon their temporary stronghold. Their eyes darted in every direction, searching for an escape route. With hearts pounding, they raced downhill, their footsteps echoing against the rugged terrain.

In the midst of smoke and flames, the police force seized the opportunity to regroup and launch a fierce pursuit of the retreating militants. Yohan, his mind solely focused on capturing Banjur, led the charge with unwavering determination. His heart thumped in his chest, a mix of adrenaline and purpose coursing through his veins. The militants, their retreat turned into a desperate escape, fired haphazardly in a last-ditch attempt to fend off their pursuers. But their shots lacked precision and planning, veering off into the night sky. Neigham, caught in the chaos, fired his weapon, unintentionally striking a fellow policeman who fell to the ground, blood seeping from his chest.

Pushkar and Yohan's spirits sank at the sight of their fallen comrade. Their eyes filled with disappointment and determination, hardened by the weight of responsibility. Yohan's attention quickly shifted from the fallen officer to Pushkar, his voice unwavering as he issued orders. "Give me cover fire, Pushkar," Yohan commanded. "I'm going to position myself near the entrance."

That's risky, sir."

"It's okay," Yohan reassured him. "The moment I see Banjur, I want to nab him. Now get that water hose I asked you to get and spill water on the pathway." Yohan recalled his carefully planned strategy. He signalled for the water hose he had previously requested. Pushkar swiftly handed it to him, and Yohan motioned for his teammates to wet the pathway ahead. Water gushed from the hose, splashing across the road's surface. The ground became slick and slippery, making the escape route a hazard for the fleeing militants. Their frantic footsteps faltered, their movements increasingly unsteady as they slipped and stumbled. Meanwhile, those militants who had already made it to the bottom of the hill scoured the area for armed policemen, intending to eliminate any threat. Shots rang out, and the forest erupted with the deafening exchange of gunfire. The police force, well-positioned and prepared, fought back with unyielding resolve.

Neigham surveyed the scene, witnessing the meticulously planned police assault unfolding before his eyes. The realisation dawned upon him swiftly - the law enforcement's relentless pursuit was solely due to Banjur's presence in their camp. He ordered his fighters to provide cover fire while he guided Banjur toward an empty police jeep parked a few hundred metres away — a getaway vehicle that held their key to freedom. Yohan's eyes darted through the chaotic scene, desperately searching for a glimpse of Banjur. Adrenaline surged within him, knowing that capturing Banjur would not only be a vital success for their mission but also a personal victory for his beloved Sukumar, who was fighting for his life in the hospital. Following the swift movements of Neigham and Banjur, Yohan pursued them with determined strides. However, he remained a considerable distance behind. Sensing Yohan closing in, urgency gripped the two militants, propelling them to quicken their pace, their eyes fixed on the police jeep that held their hopes of escape. Yohan made a calculated decision. He withheld his fire, knowing that recklessly shooting at the fleeing jeep could risk Banjur's life or lead to further chaos.

Reaching the waiting jeep, Neigham wasted no time. He swiftly ignited the engine, the roaring sound mingling with the chaotic symphony of combat. The vehicle, conveniently positioned in the direction of their intended escape route, surged forward, its wheels spinning with determination.

Banjur, his face etched with unease, glanced back and caught a glimpse of Yohan trailing behind. An uneasy feeling gnawed at him, threatening to undermine his confidence.

"Neigham, something is wrong. I can sense it," Banjur voiced his concerns, his tone laced with panic.

Neigham's eyes flickered with a hint of uncertainty, but he quickly brushed it aside. "Don't worry, sir," he responded, his voice projecting false reassurance. "We will get out of here. Just hold on tight." Neigham skilfully manoeuvred the jeep, its tires kicking up dirt and gravel as it surged forward, leaving behind a trail of uncertainty and danger. The road ahead seemed both endless and fraught with peril.

Banjur glanced back anxiously, checking if Yohan was still in pursuit. But as Neigham steered the vehicle ahead, he saw Yohan's distance increasing further. Suddenly, he noticed Yohan stop, which Neigham observed through the rearview mirror.

"I told you, Banjur sir. He won't be able to catch us. He has stopped running."

"That scares me even more," Banjur muttered, still keeping a watchful eye on Yohan. Seeing Yohan standing still, with his fists on his waist, exuding unwavering confidence, intensified the doubts racing through the militant's mind.

At that very moment, the tires screeched loudly as if they had been punctured. The vehicle jolted forward, losing control, and came to a sudden standstill.

Fear etched across the faces of the militants as their bodies lurched forward, crashing into the steering wheel and dashboard. In that split second, a wave of police officers, who had been stealthily concealed, emerged with their weapons drawn, encircling the disoriented militants. Banjur, his suspicions confirmed, knew that this was Yohan's carefully orchestrated trap.

As the realisation dawned on Banjur that it was the end of the road for him, he heard the echoing footsteps growing closer from behind, closing in on him and Neigham. Slowly, from behind, emerged the tall and imposing figure of Yohan, his presence commanding and powerful. With a triumphant smile gracing his face, Yohan stood before them, radiating a sense of victory and satisfaction.

"Sorry, Neigham, but did you believe that the Indian police would leave a vehicle conveniently waiting for you? You should have been smarter," Yohan taunted, his voice dripping with smugness. He then shifted his gaze to Banjur, the man he had relentlessly pursued.

"Come, Banjur. Now that you have witnessed our action, it's time to see our hospitality."

***

"How's he doing, Sethu *akka*?" Yohan inquired over the phone to Sethulakshmi, Sukumar's wife, who sat outside the ICU in AIMS, Delhi. The injured Sukumar had been air-lifted from Assam to Delhi with Yohan's help, pulling all the strings with Director Verma's assistance.

"The doctors said he is getting better. He asked for you when he regained consciousness, Yohan," the wife replied, her voice clouded with despair.

"I'll be there soon, *akka*."

"He would love that, Yohan."

After ending the call, his mind lingered in the hospital, concerned for Sukumar. But there was work to do, especially after capturing Banjur. The man had been a major presence in the scenes of two out of four murders and held answers to many questions. Ila and Gunang were completing their ongoing assignments, and the team was scheduled to meet at the CBI headquarters in the evening to catch up.

Yohan walked into the interrogation room where Banjur sat on a lonely chair meant to intimidate the accused. Like his previous interrogation rooms, Yohan maintained the darkness and lack of air. These discomforts were purposely inflicted to break the morale of tough nuts like Banjur.

Banjur sat in his black round-neck T-shirt and camouflage pants, dusty and sand-covered from the recent standoff with the police. Yohan knew that the man in front of him was the closest aide to Anup Baruah, whose name and organisation, ATLF, had been linked to a series of murders.

"So, Banjur," Yohan said, cutting to the chase, "… why did you and ATLF murder Mekhala, Zulekha, and Siddharth?" He deliberately left out Bollywood star Samar.

Banjur winked, "Wow, Mr. Yohan. Are you sure that's the whole list?"

Yohan was taken aback by Banjur's reaction. It was almost as if he was admitting to the allegations, but not directly.

"So, Banjur, are you admitting to the murders?" Yohan asked.

"I'm simply acknowledging all this hearsay about the murders," Banjur said.

"Of course. Why would you admit to anything when your boss, Anup Baruah, is behind all this? Just tell me why."

"Oh, Mr. Yohan," Banjur said. "Don't try to involve respectable people here. Mr. Anup is an honourable, law-abiding citizen."

"Oh, of course," Yohan said. "That's why he's been missing from the law's radar for years."

"He's very much within the boundaries of the law," Banjur said. "Your government has nothing against him."

"My government?" Yohan smiled. "I thought law-abiding citizens would say 'our Government'."

"Our country, yes. Our Government doesn't mean the same thing, Mr. Yohan."

Banjur was not your typical stereotype of a militant. He was well-spoken and articulate and seemed to be enjoying the cat-and-mouse game with Yohan. Yohan knew Banjur's statement wasn't entirely wrong, but the evidence against him made him an enemy of the state. As the interview continued, Yohan realised Banjur was more than just a foot soldier for ATLF. He was a key strategist and planner and well-versed in the group's ideology.

Yohan took out the photos that indicated Banjur's presence at the crime scenes of Mekhala and Siddharth and slammed them on the table.

"Your presence has been confirmed, Banjur," he said. "There's no escaping this for you, and there's no point in denying your organisation or Anup Baruah's role in all of this."

Banjur glanced at the photos and looked up at Yohan, "Why do you have to drag ATLF and Anup *da* into this? Is this some witch hunt against our leaders and people?"

"Oh, don't you dare play the victim card, Banjur," Yohan said.

"That's precisely the problem, Mr. Yohan," Banjur said. "Your Government protects the perpetrators and shoves all the blame onto us victims. Have you ever, for once, been open to seeing things from our perspective?"

Banjur was not the typical criminal that Yohan had interrogated before. He was a suave and calculated man, and his rebuttals were not just pointed but laden with highly sensitive issues. For the first time in his questioning, Yohan felt on the back foot. In front of him was a smart individual making strategic moves.

"I understand your confidence comes from the fact that you feel your supreme commander will protect you," Yohan said, tweaking his approach a bit.

"Oh, you really think we are some powerful people, ready to always put your beautiful country at risk, right?" Banjur lashed out. "You don't for a second consider that we are just soldiers fighting to protect our land and culture, *haan*?"

Despite his adversary's confidence, Yohan stayed calm and patient, waiting for the right moment to strike.

"Actually, I have evidence to believe that you are nothing but a textbook example of a victim affected by a clear and coldly executed organised crime," Yohan said, changing gears at the snap of his fingers.

Banjur's composure, which had been unwavering until now, began to shake.

"Okay, what's this new play, officer?" he asked.

"Actually, a good word, Banjur. It's a play, like a game of chess," Yohan said.

"We are getting all metaphorical here. Are we officer? You know I am a Literature graduate, by the way," Banjur used the opportunity to brag about his academic qualifications.

"Well, I wish it was a metaphor, but you are in a game of chess, and sadly, you are just a pawn," Yohan said.

"Come on, officer. You're bluffing."

Yohan's eyes narrowed. "Am I?" he asked. "We'll see about that."

"Okay, hit me with your best theory, Mr. Yohan."

Yohan loved it when his opponents assumed a sense of overconfidence, recognising it as the moment to get one step ahead of them. He smiled a predatory smile that made Banjur's blood run cold. "The thing is, Banjur," he said, "… you now find yourself in a very unique situation."

"What do you mean?"

"In a very strange way, you are a victim of your own actions." Yohan's face had a weird energy on it.

Banjur's face paled. "And how so, officer?" he asked, the conviction in his voice fading.

Yohan reached into his file and pulled out a photo. It was a photo of Zulekha. He held it up in front of Banjur's face.

"This is one of the people who was killed, and I am sure you have a role in it. Maybe not directly, but somehow."

"You are spinning some wild story here, Mr. Yohan," Banjur said, still not sure where this was headed.

"Okay, okay. I want you to see one of the many reasons why Zulekha was killed. Trust me, even you don't know this," Yohan said, producing a newspaper cutting that Gunang had uncovered during their investigation into Zulekha's past as a journalist.

Banjur examined the cutting closely and angrily flicked it away, making it land on the floor. "This is absolute fucking bullshit," he screamed.

"I know this changes everything for you, Banjur. But this is the truth," Yohan replied calmly.

"Why the fuck should I believe you? I have strong reasons to think otherwise," Banjur raised his voice. "I have my whole fucking life to believe otherwise."

Ignoring Banjur's outburst, Yohan reached for the file again, pulled out a few pieces of paper bearing incriminating evidence, and spread them on the table for Banjur to see. The militant, who had always felt one step ahead, finally realised why Yohan had remained as cool as ice during the whole proceeding. A state of shock washed over Banjur as he saw his whole life fall apart before his eyes, unable to comprehend the intensity of his emotions in the face of the damning evidence.

"This is why I said that you are just a pawn and, quite unusually, the biggest victim of all your crimes," Yohan explained, leaving copies of the evidence for Banjur to process the information. Without another word, he got up and walked away, the silent noise of Banjur's cries ringing in his ears as he moved further from the supposedly dangerous militant.

Chapter 16
A LEAD IN TIME SAVES INVESTIGATION TIME

Yohan entered his cabin with sweat on his brow, still panting and gasping for breath after taking the stairs to the 7th floor of the CBI headquarters. The elevator was out of order, but that didn't deter him. He was a man of action, and nothing could slow him down, especially when the stakes were high.

In the room, Ila and Gunang were already engrossed in their findings, poring over documents and evidence that could break the case wide open. Gunang, the newest member of the team, had an eager and determined look in her eyes. She had fought hard to be here, rising from a humble village in Assam to become a part of the prestigious CBI. For her, every assignment was an opportunity to prove herself, and she was ready to give it her all.

"Ila, what did you find?" Yohan managed to ask between breaths, his focus unwavering despite his physical exertion.

"I also found something very interesting about Samar and another peculiar connection to the case," Gunang chimed in with enthusiasm. However, she couldn't help feeling a bit uncertain among her more experienced colleagues. She wanted to make her mark and prove that she belonged here.

Yohan's eyes darted between Ila and Gunang, especially fixated on the latter's face, filled with dedication and determination. He had been in her shoes before, the new member of a tight-knit team, and he knew how important it was to support and encourage them.

"Good job, Gunang," Yohan said, his voice warm and encouraging. "Your breakthrough about Zulekha helped break Banjur."

Gunang's face lit up with pride, and a genuine smile spread across her lips. The praise from her leader meant the world to her, and it instilled a newfound sense of confidence.

"Thank you, Yohan sir."

"Call me Yohan. No 'sir' needed."

"Sure," Gunang replied, her shoulders feeling light.

Ila smiled, understanding Yohan's intent to foster a welcoming and supportive environment for the new member of the team. She had been there, too, and knew the value of such gestures.

"Go ahead, Gunang. What did you find?" Ila prompted.

Gunang took a deep breath, her fingers trembling slightly as she opened her laptop to display the records, "I investigated Zulekha thoroughly since she is the only one who connects the dots between Mekhala, Samar, and Siddharth. She has something to do with all of them."

"Yeah, she was Samar's yoga instructor whom Siddharth introduced the actor to," Yohan recalled, leaning forward with keen interest. "And because she was receiving payments from Trilok publishers, we know that she had something connecting her to Mekhala."

"But we don't have a concrete link as of now," Ila cut in, her voice heavy with disappointment.

"Based on my investigation, there is more than what meets the eye," Gunang continued, her attention shifting between Yohan and Ila. "So, it turns out Zulekha may not have been just a yoga instructor to Samar."

The room was silent, the only sound was the faint ticking of a clock. Gunang's words hung in the air, heavy with possibilities. Yohan's mind raced, connections spinning through his head. They were close; he knew it. They were close to uncovering something big.

"These murders have taken place one year after the other, starting with Zulekha and followed by Samar. So, I made a calculated hypothesis that the first two people who were murdered could be immediate threats," Gunang's voice trembled with excitement.

"Yes, that makes sense," Ila agreed, her eyes narrowing as she began to connect the dots.

"So, of course, as Yohan had instructed, I looked into Zulekha's connection to Banjur and ATLF. Then I looked into what connection Samar had with ATLF," Gunang continued, her fingers typing furiously on the keyboard.

"Keep going, Gunang. Looks like you are onto something here," Yohan urged, his eyes locking onto Gunang's.

Gunang nodded, her fingers flying across the keyboard. "Well, it turns out that one of Mekhala's colleagues had met with Samar before his murder," she said, her voice tinged with excitement.

Yohan's eyes narrowed, "Don't tell me it's Preetam Gowda," he said, a flicker of excitement crossing his face since the missing author was already in their custody.

"Unfortunately, no, Yohan," Gunang replied and then continued, "... so this author named MR Shaikh met with Samar just a few months before his murder."

"But just meeting Samar can't be your only reason to doubt him," Yohan questioned, intrigued by the new lead.

"Of course, apart from the fact that he was Mekhala's author," Ila reminded.

"To answer all your questions, let me give you some more context," Gunang started explaining. She pulled out her laptop and displayed some newspaper reports from that time on Samar.

"So these are some newspaper articles from around that time," Gunang said, pointing to the screen of her laptop.

"Anything unusual?" Yohan asked.

"So around that time, there was a lot of news about Samar signing a new project based on this book by MR Shaikh," Gunang added and placed a copy of the book on the table.

"But who is this MR Shaikh, and what is his novel about?" Ila asked, her interest growing.

"So that's the thing. Shaikh worked as a journalist in the same area as Zulekha and around the same time. Of course, I don't have any leads connecting Zulekha to him yet," Gunang added with a hint of frustration.

"Were you able to get in touch with him, Gunang?" Ila asked, hoping to find a breakthrough.

"No, not yet, Ila. But I did read summaries on this book."

As they spoke, Ila noticed Yohan browsing through the book, and a sly smile appeared on his lips, indicating he had come across something intriguing. Even as Gunang spoke, Ila couldn't control her curiosity and turned to Yohan. "What is it, Yohan?"

Yohan raised his eyebrows, and with a slight grin, he said, "It's interesting. Something that has been on my mind for a long time finally gets closure today." After saying this, he walked to their evidence board and pointed to a name that had crossed paths of this investigation and remained mysterious so far.

Seeing it, Ila quickly turned the pages of her diary to get to the page with the name, and her eyes widened with disbelief. She asked, "Is it the same person?"

Even though it was her finding, Gunang was lost seeing this covert conversation between her two colleagues and interrupted, "What is it, guys?"

"So when we were interrogating Adinarayan in the beginning, he happened to mention a name… a person after meeting whom Mekhala was very disturbed," Yohan recalled.

"Mustafa Shaikh," Ila proclaimed, her memory connecting the dots.

"And as we know now, this could be the same person… MR Shaikh or Mustafa Riaz Shaikh," Yohan said, displaying the book's back cover with the author's bio.

"But none of Mekhala's publishers knew this Mustafa Sheikh. Remember, we asked?" Ila sought clarification.

"That's because this book is self-published. Mekhala probably was saving this as the movie would have made more impact. The deaths of Zulekha and Siddharth would have made her cautious," Yohan replied.

The room crackled with tension as the team digested the latest revelation. Their mission had just escalated to a heart-pounding level. Finding Mustafa Shaikh became paramount, and they needed to protect him at all costs, as he could be a crucial witness in the whole scheme of things.

"There is a story shaping up, a motive slowly showing itself in this crazy case," Yohan told his teammates.

"Yes, Yohan. This hopefully takes us one step closer to Banjur's boss, who is hiding in the shadows," Ila pointed out. While Yohan focused on the motive, Ila made it a point to remind everyone that catching the real culprit was equally crucial.

Gunang, who was listening intently, felt a surge of determination, "Let's find Mustafa Shaikh before ATLF does. He might hold the key to unravelling everything and bringing the culprits to justice.

Yohan's voice cut like a knife through the tension, "Ila, call in every favour, every connection. We need eyes and ears everywhere, monitoring every corner. I want Mustafa Shaikh here."

Suddenly, Yohan saw his phone ring on the table. It was Sukumar's wife. Usually, Yohan would not take personal calls while in a meeting, even if it was his father's. But his heart felt heavy seeing Sethulakshmi's name flashing on the screen. Fear gripped Yohan's heart like a vise, his mind torn between his duty and the fear of unwelcome news about Sukumar.

Yohan excused himself from the intense huddle and walked to a corner, answering the call with a trembling voice, "Sethu *akka*, is everything alright?"

Her voice choked with emotion, Sethulakshmi replied, "Yohan, it's Sukumar. He regained consciousness."

On hearing this, Yohan's eyes shed tears as he was overjoyed to hear it. His colleague, rather his elder brother, had woken up from danger. "What did the doctors say, *akka*?"

"He is getting better, Yohan. He spoke to me a little," Even though it was good news, Sethulakshmi's voice still trembled.

Relief washed over Yohan as he heard the words he desperately longed for. Sukumar was awake, and there was hope. "Thank the heavens! I'll be there right away," he replied, his voice filled with emotion.

"Yohan, hold on for a moment," she said, trying to steady her trembling voice.

"Why, *akka*?"

"Because when he woke up," Sethulakshmi replied, "… the first thing he said was to give his phone to you, and he used the words 'Sukumar sollre'."

"*Sollre*… what does it mean?" Yohan inquired eagerly.

"In Tamil, 'sollre' means 'says'," Sethulakshmi explained. "I've already sent Sukumar's phone to my brother. He'll be reaching the CBI headquarters soon."

"That's incredible, Sethu. And don't you worry, our Sukumar will be fit and back soon."

Yohan couldn't help but feel a sense of pride for his partner. Even in his injured state, Sukumar's unwavering commitment to his duty and passion for justice shone through. It was one of the many reasons why Yohan admired him so much.

As he kept the phone, Yohan couldn't help but glance at the entrance from the balcony, eagerly waiting for Sethulakshmi's brother to arrive with the parcel. The anticipation was overwhelming, and Yohan could feel the weight of the moment. He knew that if Sukumar stressed the importance of sending the phone even in his current state, then whatever was in that device could potentially hold a crucial clue they were looking for.

****

The tension in the air was palpable as Yohan, Ila, and Gunang huddled together in Yohan's dimly lit cabin. Time seemed to slow down as Yohan's fingers danced across Sukumar's phone, navigating through app after app, searching for a clue that could open the case.

His heart pounded in his chest as he stumbled upon Sukumar's email. With bated breath, he opened the drafts folder, and there it was – a trail of emails, all saved with the enigmatic subject line, "Sukumar *Sollre.*" Yohan's instincts told him this could be the key they had desperately sought.

Eager to reveal the potential breakthrough, Yohan connected the phone to his computer, projecting the screen for Ila and Gunang. The glow from the computer screen flickered, illuminating their faces with an eerie intensity.

One by one, Yohan opened the emails, eyes scanning the contents with laser-like focus. The messages contained various details of the investigation, but nothing screamed out as the missing piece of the puzzle.

In a feverish frenzy, Yohan meticulously scrutinised every email. The silence in the room was broken only by the soft hum of the computer and the occasional hushed whispers between the three investigators. Time seemed to blur as they delved deeper into Sukumar's digital world.

Just when a wave of frustration threatened to overtake Yohan, his eyes locked onto one of the most recent emails.

The mail had the names of all four victims, but their eyes were fixated on the intriguing sequence of numbers next to each victim's name.

Zulekha - 0765427 (AEC)
Samar - 0865432 (AEC)
Siddharth - 0456789 (AEC)
Mekhala - 0387654 (AEC)

"What are these numbers?" Gunang asked, her voice tinged with curiosity and excitement.

Yohan's gaze remained fixed on the screen, his mind racing as he deciphered the cryptic clue. "Look carefully," he said, his voice steady but full of urgency, "... the clue is hidden in this itself."

Ila's instincts kicked in, and she immediately grasped the significance of the numbers. Her eyes widened with realisation. "This is amazing," she exclaimed, her voice trembling with excitement. "This proves the connection we were looking for. Sukumar, you resourceful genius."

Gunang, who hadn't been part of the investigation from the beginning, sought clarification. "Wait, can someone tell me what this is all about?"

"Of course, Gunang," Yohan began explaining. "So, we had earlier found that Zulekha and Siddharth had a military connection."

"Military? But women can't serve in combat roles in the Indian army. So what was she then?" Gunang inquired.

"Yeah, so. They were not in the army, but they had written the exam and didn't clear it," Ila clarified.

"Still, what is the connection?" Gunang remained puzzled.

"So, Gunang, here are two photos," Yohan retrieved the mysterious photos they had found in Zulekha and Samar's houses. At that moment, a wave of shock washed over Gunang's face. She hadn't seen these before, and she could identify one common person in both of them. Even then, Gunang couldn't entirely comprehend the exact connection, but the significance of the photos started to dawn on her as she listened to Ila and Yohan explain.

"And, Gunang, you're right. Opportunities for women in the army were limited back then," Yohan remarked as he pulled out Sukumar's phone. "And that's precisely why the 'AEC' written in brackets next to their names make sense... the Army Education Corps."

The Army Education Corps (AEC) was created in 1921 to address the issue of many Indian soldiers not knowing how to read or write. As a special part of the Indian Army, the AEC focuses on teaching soldiers and their families, offering education before, during, and after their military service. The role of the AEC was not just to help soldiers improve their job skills but also their lives in general.

After a rapid overview of the AEC's role, Yohan rose from his seat, a spark of determination in his eyes. He reached for the files of each victim and placed them deliberately in front of his colleagues, Ila and Gunang. "Now, do you notice any other common threads among the murdered individuals?" Yohan posed the question.

"They all took the AEC exam in 2014," Gunang responded quickly.

"A good starting point, but let's dig deeper," Yohan encouraged.

"They all fell within the age range of 23 to 26 when they took the exam. Siddharth was 23, while both Zulekha and Samar were 24. Mekhala was 26," Gunang persisted in her efforts.

"Again, well done, Gunang. You're nearly there. The age eligibility for AEC exams is between 22 and 27," Yohan confirmed, nodding appreciatively.

As Gunang leaned into the speed of her analysis, Ila delved deeper into the files, her mind racing to forge a stronger connection. Suddenly, realisation dawned upon her, and she interjected, "All of them have completed at least a master's degree in education."

Yohan's palms hit the table with a resounding thud, as if an epiphany had surged through him. "Exactly, Ila. You're almost there!" his voice carried a mix of excitement and certainty.

"A quick google search tells me that candidates interested in joining the AEC must possess a master's degree in any discipline with at least 50% marks. If they meet this criteria, then they must go through a written exam and an interview, " Ila added.

"Indeed," Yohan continued with fervour. "Now, we must delve into their lives. Four highly qualified individuals were rejected by the Army at the interview stage, followed by each pursuing a different career path, only to be met with death. The only commonality among them is that they attempted the exam in the same year and faced rejection," Yohan's voice echoed with a sense of unfolding intrigue.

"And don't forget the Assam connection in their cases," Ila pointed out, her eyes gleaming with determination.

"Except for Samar," Gunang chimed in.

"Actually, the connection to MR Shaikh established Samar's Assam link as well," Yohan clarified.

"But, Yohan, the man in the photo still puzzles me. What do we do about that?" Gunang's query reflected her genuine concern.

"That's the next step, Gunang. Don't worry. But before we dive into that, Ila, you were supposed to update us on what you got from Adinarayan," Yohan's memory resurfaced suddenly.

"Oh, I almost forgot. This case is taking so many turns that I nearly overlooked the most crucial lead," Ila lamented, rapidly retrieving her notes.

"What is it?" Gunang's impatience was palpable.

"Remember Shweta revealing that Adinarayan was the one who informed her about Zulekha's involvement?"

"Yes," Yohan and Gunang replied in tandem.

"Well, it turns out that someone dearly connected to our case fed that information to Adinarayan," Ila divulged.

"Who?" Yohan's curiosity brimmed.

Ila scribbled a name onto a piece of paper, and in a room already awash with unexpected revelations and newfound information, this name intensified the prevailing sense of intrigue.

"I think I have a vague idea of what's transpiring, but we need to update Director Verma. It's time we confront the truth," Yohan's words carried the urgency of a battle cry. Without further delay, he retrieved his cell phone and dialled Director Verma's number. The conversation began with Yohan quickly briefing Verma on the team's findings.

After intently listening, Director Verma fell into contemplation, his pause lasting a few pregnant seconds.

Weighing the options, he finally decided to elevate the stakes. "Yohan, Ila, and Gunang, brace yourselves. Let's meet the Prime Minister of India tomorrow."

Chapter 17

THE ONE WHERE YOU FIND OUT WHAT BEFORE WHO

In the pulsating heart of New Delhi, cradled amidst the sprawling, meticulously manicured lawns of Race Course Road, the Prime Minister's residence stood proudly. A symbol of power and elegance, it was a cornerstone of Indian polity. The sun draped its golden hues over the sandstone walls, accentuating the grandeur of the estate, imbuing it with an almost ethereal glow.

Yohan led the ensemble with a determined stride, accompanied by Director Verma, Ila and Gunang. As they traversed the majestic hallways of the residence, their footsteps reverberated against the polished marble floors. Each step seemed to carry the weight of their formidable task, echoing through the corridors of power. The walls around them were a tapestry of India's rich cultural heritage, adorned with exquisite paintings and sculptures that whispered stories of bygone eras. The air was laced with a delicate fragrance of jasmine, casting an almost surreal quality to the atmosphere, as if they were walking through a dream.

They navigated the security protocols with practised ease, moving through multiple checkpoints with a solemn air. The security personnel, clad in crisp, impeccable uniforms, examined every badge and scrutinised every face with unwavering attention to detail, their eyes sharp and unyielding.

With each advancing step towards the Prime Minister's office, the weight of their mission seemed to grow heavier, more tangible. Feeling the gravity of the moment, Yohan subtly adjusted his collar, a subconscious gesture to fortify himself against the challenges ahead. Beside him, Director Verma wore an inscrutable expression, but his eyes betrayed a razor-sharp focus, like a predator zeroing in on its prey. With a furrowed brow, Ila glanced over her notes one final time, ensuring that no detail, however minute, had escaped her scrutiny. Gunang surveyed their surroundings with a vigilant gaze, more excited than worried, as it was her first time in this magnificent structure of India's political landscape.

As they reached the heavy teak door of the Prime Minister's office, they paused, each lost in their thoughts yet united in their purpose. They took a deep, steadying breath. Beyond this threshold lay the answers they had been tirelessly seeking and, perhaps, questions they hadn't yet dared to contemplate.

With a shared nod, they stepped forward, crossing into a realm where every decision could alter the course of their investigation or history itself.

As the team stepped inside, the atmosphere shifted noticeably. They were immediately greeted by the Prime Minister's personal assistant, Mr. Ekun Sharma, who embodied both professionalism and cordiality. "Good morning, Director Verma," he said with a respectful nod. "The Honourable Prime Minister will meet you in five minutes," his voice, a mix of reverence and efficiency, guided the team into the meeting room.

Upon entering, they found themselves in a space that exuded elegance and authority. The room was spacious, its layout meticulously organised. Dominating the setting was a single red sofa, majestic and unmistakably reserved for the Prime Minister. Complementing it were two three-seater sofas, symmetrically arranged across a sleek glass table, setting the stage for discussions of National importance.

The room's walls were adorned with towering bookshelves, serving as custodians of wisdom. They housed an impressive collection of books, including the revered Constitution of India. The spines of these books displayed a rich tapestry of knowledge.

In one corner, two single seaters and a small table were neatly arranged, a dedicated spot for note-takers, the silent observers of history in the making. Although the Prime Minister was not yet present, his influence was evident in every detail of the room, from the strategic placement of the furniture to the charged atmosphere that seemed to echo with the weight of decisions shaping the Nation.

The team's gaze momentarily settled on the floral red carpet that covered the floor. Each thread seemed to hold the memory of the numerous dignitaries and decision-makers who had traversed this room.

As the members of the team took their respective seats, they each drew a deep breath, mentally preparing for the encounter ahead. The anticipation in the room was thick, a blend of respect and the thrill of the unknown. They were on the cusp of meeting the supremo, a pivotal figure not only in their investigation but in the lifeblood of the nation. With each passing second, the anticipation grew, heightening the sense of significance as they awaited the arrival of one of the most powerful individuals in the country.

Suddenly, the room was jolted into heightened alertness as the door swung open with a resonant thud. This sharp and commanding sound snapped everyone inside to immediate attention.

Accompanied by a cadre of SPG officers, the Prime Minister made his entrance. He was dressed in a peach-checkered long kurta paired with pristine white pyjamas, an embodiment of traditional elegance. His eyes, sharp and discerning, quickly scanned the room, taking in the faces of those present with a practised ease. The SPG officers, silent and imposing, took their positions at the various gates and strategically behind the sofa. There was a sense of choreographed precision in their movements, a silent testament to their unwavering vigilance.

Without hesitation, the Prime Minister occupied his seat on the red sofa, the central piece of the room that seemed to have been waiting just for him. With a subtle gesture, he indicated for the officers in front of him to take their seats, a silent command that was promptly obeyed.

Ekun Sharma, the PA, swiftly approached the Prime Minister, ready to introduce the visitors. "Sir, this is Jagat Verma, the CBI director, and this is his team," he began.

But before he could finish, the Prime Minister interjected, his voice carrying a confident, knowing tone, "Ekun *ji*, of course, I know him. We have met many times officially." His interruption was not abrupt but seemed to flow naturally, a sign of his familiarity with high-stakes meetings.

Turning his attention to Director Verma, the Prime Minister's demeanour was one of serious inquisition. "So, tell me, sir. What is this urgent matter?" he asked, his voice direct and expectant.

With a measured gesture, Director Verma placed his hand on Yohan's shoulder, "Sir, this is Yohan Tytler, the investigation lead. He will brief you."

The Prime Minister's eyes twinkled with recognition at the mention of the name. "Tytler. That name reminds me of one person," he said with a light smile, bridging the formal gap with a touch of familiarity.

"I am his son, sir. But I assure you, he had nothing to do with me being a CBI officer," Yohan responded, eager to establish his own identity in this high-stakes scenario.

"I must assume so. Why would a cement tycoon worth billions want his son in a government job?" the Prime Minister jested, lightening the mood with humour.

"He loves cement, and I love justice," Yohan replied, his voice carrying a sense of pride in his chosen path, distinct from his father's.

"Anyway, tell me, Mr. Tytler," the Prime Minister gestured, signalling for the briefing to begin.

Yohan nodded to Ila, who promptly handed him the files. Passing one to the Prime Minister, he stated, "From the beginning, this case has been shrouded in mystery, even in its allotment to me, sir. It also involved the opposition using your name as a suspect."

"Yes, yes. Kailash *ji* never spares any opportunity, but he is a good man and a friend," the Prime Minister acknowledged, showing his awareness of the political undercurrents.

"So, sir, it started with the death of Mekhala Thampi, a literary agent and someone who had met you a week before her death," Yohan continued.

"I know Mekhala *ji*," the Prime Minister confirmed, his expression turning more solemn.

"Sir, why did she meet you?" Ila unexpectedly interjected, breaking protocol. Gunang, taken aback by her audacity, exchanged a surprised glance with Director Verma, but Yohan wasn't fazed by her boldness.

"Madam, let the briefing happen, and I will disclose," the Prime Minister answered calmly.

Neither Yohan nor Ila seemed fully satisfied with the answer, but Yohan decided to proceed with the briefing.

"Investigating Mekhala's murder, we came across three more murders and several disappearances that seemed linked to the crime," Yohan began. "Zulekha, a corporate employee and yoga teacher in 2019; the very beloved Bollywood star Samar in 2020; Siddharth, an MNC HR recruiter in 2021; and of course, Mekhala in 2022."

As Yohan spoke, the Prime Minister listened intently, nodding occasionally, while Ila's gaze remained fixed on him, scrutinising his every reaction.

"Sir, we identified several cross-linkages between these people. Zulekha and Siddharth were friends. Siddharth introduced Zulekha to Samar, and she became his yoga instructor. We also have evidence to believe Zulekha had some connections to Mekhala, and one of Mekhala's client's books was going to be made into a film starring Samar," Yohan continued, unfolding the complex web of connections in the case.

"But is there anything connecting all these murders?" the Prime Minister inquired.

In response, Yohan gestured to Ila, encouraging her to take the lead. He believed firmly in the collective strength of his team and the importance of recognising each member's contributions. Director Verma observed this exchange with a knowing smile, recognising he had chosen the right man to lead this intricate investigation.

"Two and a half connections, Mr. Prime Minister," Ila began with confidence.

"Oh wow! I must say, I am more curious about the half," the Prime Minister remarked, his interest visibly piqued.

"Actually, sir, the half is why we are here," Ila replied, her composure unwavering. She continued, "The first common connection is that these four were military aspirants but failed the Army Education Corps exams in the same year, that is, 2014. The second connection is with Assam, specifically, the ATLF."

"You mean Anup Baruah has something to do with all this? This is a very serious allegation, and it points to a very sensitive area for the country," the Prime Minister warned, his tone reflecting the gravity of the situation.

"Absolutely, sir. But we have nabbed one of ATLF's main men, Banjur, who has confessed to these murders," Ila informed confidently.

"And what's the half?" the Prime Minister asked, his curiosity reaching its peak.

Seizing the moment, Yohan presented a set of photos, specifically those of Zulekha and Mekhala, with one common individual that the team had retrieved. The Prime Minister scanned the pictures carefully, his eyes widening as he recognised the common person in them, realisation dawning upon him about the direction in which this briefing was heading.

"And for this briefing to continue, we need your permission," Yohan stated, the implication clear and significant.

The Prime Minister, visibly absorbed by the revelations, rose from his seat and walked over to Ekun Sharma. He whispered something into his PA's ear, "Ask him to meet us in the next 15 minutes." The urgency and importance of the situation were evident in his swift actions, indicating the briefing was about to take an even more critical turn.

****

The room, now with an additional member, maintained its quiet intensity. Each individual sat firmly in their seat, a silent acknowledgement of the gravity of the situation. The new entrant, occupying the couch opposite the CBI team, was none other than Arvind Shankar, the Home Minister.

Acting as a bridge between the two parties, the Prime Minister initiated the dialogue. "So, Arvind *ji*, Director Verma and his team need some clarifications from you." This introduction set the stage for what was to be a crucial part of the investigation.

Since the Home Minister was about to be summoned, Verma had suggested that Ila and Gunang remain outside due to the sensitive nature of the discussion. However, Yohan had insisted on their inclusion. After a brief negotiation, it was decided that Ila would stay as she was senior, while Gunang would wait outside.

After a quick survey of the room, Arvind Shankar directed his attention to Yohan, "Mr. Tytler, I thought I told you to come to me first when you find something. This is clearly an act of insubordination. You, too, Verma, have disappointed me," he chided.

Despite the heat of the moment, Verma stood up for his team, "Sir, I always kept you in the loop, but when your involvement in the case became apparent, it put us in a challenging position."

"Okay, Verma. Tell me what makes me your suspect," the Home Minister demanded.

Yohan took the lead in responding, "Actually, sir, we are yet to establish you as a suspect. But you have a solid connection to this case. You knew that when you assigned me to it."

"Hmm, okay, Tytler. What have you got on me?" the minister probed.

"This all started with you. I have a theory, and I need you to fill in the rest," Yohan stated, ready to summarise his findings.

The Prime Minister, eager to expedite the process, urged, "Please go ahead, Mr. Tytler."

Yohan began to unveil the narrative, "After you became the Home Minister, you thoroughly assessed all national security threats. One of the most significant threats was the ATLF, led by Anup Baruah. It represented a major conflict that could destabilise the entire region."

He continued, "It was in 2014 that the current government came into power. India was facing insurgencies in several parts, incited by our volatile neighbours like Pakistan and China, who aimed to create unrest. The ATLF, with aspirations for an independent land, posed a significant challenge to India's self-defence policy. While they actively recruited locals, much of their efforts were financially supported by extremist elements from China, with clear ulterior motives."

As Yohan unfolded the complex geopolitical web, the room's atmosphere grew increasingly charged, every word adding a new layer to the intricate tapestry of national security and political intrigue.

"But of course, you knew that people could be misguided, and while every Indian loves his country, these malevolent forces could go to any extent to turn people to their side," Yohan acknowledged. "So you devised a rather clever plan, leveraging one of India's greatest strengths in a way it had never been used before."

Arvind Shankar, the Home Minister, had a gentle smile on his face, sharing a knowing glance with the Prime Minister.

"I thought I was going to be accused, Tytler. But here you are, singing praises," Arvind remarked with a wry smile. "Go on. I'm intrigued to know what plan you think I made."

"Of course, sir. You began scouting for special individuals with unique skills but preferred to keep this initiative informal," Yohan continued. "You needed people with military aspirations and academic intellect, yet they had to appear as regular, unassuming individuals. So, you chose the Army Education Corps, which was being phased out and was eventually discontinued in 2017. These exams required a master's degree and an intent to teach. Since the Corps was closing, you aimed to utilise the brightest and best for a more crucial mission. These people, while never able to reveal their true identities, played a vital role in protecting not just our country's security but also its culture and history," Yohan's explanation was detailed and methodical.

The Home Minister interjected, his tone a blend of arrogance and pride. "You know, Tytler, I've heard a lot of good things about you, but I was also warned about your penchant for over-explaining. Get to the point, officer."

"Sure, sir," Yohan replied and turned to Ila. "Ila, why don't you take over for a while?" He took a sip of water, preparing for the next phase of the briefing.

"Yes, Yohan," Ila began. "As Yohan mentioned, special people with special skills. Mekhala, a literary agent influencing the nation's narrative through books. Zulekha, a yoga instructor, propagating one of India's most significant cultural strengths. Samar, a Bollywood actor—cinema is a powerful medium to influence and spread culture. Siddharth, a recruiter, focusing on employing young students, using education to wield influence." She paused, letting the implication of her words sink in. "Yoga, cinema, literature, education - peaceful, enriching sectors, but how are they utilised in combat or warfare?"

The Prime Minister and the Home Minister exchanged confident smiles, then looked at Yohan.

Yohan added, "You know, there's a term that students learn in social studies around the 8th or 9th grade. Something we've always understood theoretically, but you, Honourable

Minister, found a practical implementation for it. 'Soft Power' – India's soft power." His statement not only connected the dots but also highlighted the innovative strategy at play, one that utilised the nation's cultural and intellectual assets in a global arena.

Soft power is the ability of a country to influence others through cultural, diplomatic, and historical appeal rather than by using force or money. It's about attracting and co-opting rather than coercing or bribing. Soft power lies in a country's attractiveness and comes from things like its culture, political values, and foreign policies.

India's soft power is significant and multifaceted. It comes from its rich cultural heritage, Bollywood films, music, books, cuisine, and its contributions to global arts and literature. Yoga and traditional practices like Ayurveda have also enhanced India's soft power, promoting health and wellness worldwide. Moreover, India's democratic ideals and its role in international peacekeeping have been influential. Its large diasporic community further extends its cultural and economic influence globally. Through these avenues, India has been able to create a positive image and exert a unique and powerful influence on the world stage.

Maintaining his composure, Yohan continued, "And now comes my theory, sir. While soft power is typically employed in a global context, you adapted it for local use. You established a sort of 'SOFT POWER SQUAD' of these special individuals. I assume you deployed them to troubled areas, using India's cultural and social strengths to ensure that people targeted by external threats remain connected to our land and its values." His explanation revealed the depth of his investigation. "Based on our findings, these individuals were positioned in Assam to counteract the cultural influence of the ATLF."

Intrigued, the prime minister asked, "Okay, how did you crack this?"

"Are you agreeing to it, sir?" Yohan replied with a slight smile, his confidence evident.

"Stop being cocky, Yohan, and answer the Prime Minister," Verma gently scolded, redirecting the focus.

"Sir, there were several indicators," Yohan gestured to Ila. "Ila, please show the presentation."

Ila took over seamlessly. "We analysed the types of books Mekhala commissioned. They are all connected to India's history, politics, the significance of Assam, and its culture. A pattern emerged, suggesting a strategy to use literature to influence young minds. The self-published book by Mustafa Shaikh, set to be adapted into a film starring Samar, focused on Assam. Zulekha, as a journalist, wrote extensively about the ATLF and its repercussions for India, particularly in Assamese media."

"But what about Siddharth? What was his connection?" Arvind inquired, focusing on the missing link.

"That was something my smart boss cracked, and it was no easy feat," Ila replied, nodding towards Yohan.

With a hint of humour, Yohan said, "Ah, you're being too kind, Ila."

Arvind, growing impatient with the pleasantries, pressed, "Okay, if this mutual admiration is over, can you get to the point?"

"So, in Siddharth's case, we noticed his recruitment efforts were centred around seven universities. Two in Assam, three in Mumbai, and one each in Calcutta and Tamil Nadu. After researching these institutions, one common factor stood out," Yohan explained.

"Which was?" Arvind asked.

"They all had partnerships with Confucius Institutes," Yohan revealed.

Confucius Institutes established by China in various countries, are collaborative ventures between Chinese educational institutions and universities abroad, ostensibly to promote the Chinese language and culture globally. Operated by the Hanban, which is directly funded by the Chinese Ministry of Education, these institutes have been a focal point of China's cultural outreach. These operations to enhance China's soft power were not just an occurrence in India but also countries like the United States and the United Kingdom.

"You knew these institutes posed a significant threat, as China's intentions of promoting them worldwide, including India, are quite evident," Yohan added.

"And this leads to the broader threat you were countering – the influence of China in our local environment. Siddharth's strategic deployment was to ensure no active strategy was being used to mislead our youth," Yohan concluded his analysis.

"So, summarise your theory, Tytler," Arvind instructed.

"Simply put, sir, India was combating a form of cultural warfare or soft power war from China. They were using insurgencies like the ATLF to further their agenda, turning our people against us. I suspect ATLF is just one piece of this larger puzzle, with similar squads deployed across the country," Yohan responded.

Arvind rose from his seat and walked over to the Prime Minister, "I told you, sir. He was the right man for this job." Turning to Yohan and Ila, he complimented, "Good job, guys. But there's a small problem."

"What is it, sir?" Verma interjected, his curiosity apparent.

"I can answer that, sir," Yohan confidently stepped in, "The problem is that our honourable ministers already knew everything we shared just now before assigning us this case."

"Right, young man," the Prime Minister affirmed.

"Then why not tell us all this from the start, sir?" Verma asked.

"Well, Verma, sir," Ila interjected, "… they wanted to test if an investigation team could unravel something so confidential. If we could follow the trail, so could our enemies, potentially identifying the people involved."

"Exactly, Ms. Qureshi. This case was not just about identifying the culprits but also about helping the government strengthen this program and identifying loopholes to protect our other officers. And you've all been quite impressive," Arvind acknowledged, sparing no praise for the team's astute handling of the investigation.

"But the job is still only half done. What about the culprits? Who killed our agents?" The Prime Minister's voice carried a sense of urgency and determination.

"Sir, that is the next part of our investigation," Yohan affirmed, his gaze shifting to Ila, signalling for her to continue with the intricate narrative. "We've traced the path and discovered that while these agents were intended for non-combat roles, something went terribly wrong. These agents were effectively carrying out their duties," Yohan explained. "Mekhala was commissioning the right books and Literature. Samar was preparing for a movie about the role of the Chinese in the Assam insurgency and their use of the ATLF to create tensions. Siddharth was quietly ensuring that no university student got misguided and roped into being inside agents for China, lured by money. Zulekha pursued her journalism, actively writing on the ATLF while also using her expertise to spread the magnanimity of Indian culture through yoga. They were all being compensated through companies you had established, like Trilok Publishers and Pucolite Industries."

"Ahh, the companies were also a giveaway," Arvind acknowledged with a nod.

"Anyway, while all this was happening, Zulekha stumbled upon a crucial piece of news… a story she pursued and which eventually led to her and her teammates' deaths. It was possibly a story that could have altered the course of India's history and threatened our national security," Yohan stated gravely.

"Mr. Prime Minister, the details and the *modus operandi* behind the murders are not only shocking, but we are sitting on a ticking time bomb," Yohan added, his tone underscoring the criticality of the situation.

"So, what are we waiting for?" the Prime Minister inquired.

"Sir, your permission to arrest the culprits and present them before you," Yohan confirmed, his stance firm, reflecting the readiness to act.

"Go ahead, Tytler. Let's put an end to this, once and for all."

Chapter 18

THE ONE WHERE YOU FIND OUT HOW AND WHO

Under the veil of dusk, Yohan and his team approached a grand villa on the outskirts of Vasant Vihar. This luxurious building, masquerading as the residence of affluent non-resident Indians, was, in truth, a CBI safe house specifically chosen for its blend of opulence and secrecy. The expansive and imposing villa was hidden behind high walls and dense greenery, offering both privacy and an air of normalcy. Its well-manicured garden and elegant architectural design belied the intense activities that took place within its confines.

As they entered the villa, the team was greeted by policemen disguised as housekeepers, who were strategically positioned throughout the premises. Their casual attire was a clever cover for the seriousness of their duty, ensuring the safety and confidentiality of the operations within.

Inside, the Prime Minister and the Home Minister were present, their faces etched with anticipation and resolve. Alongside them was a group of individuals whose identities were shrouded in mystery. These select few, neither officials nor aides, were the suspects or culprits in the investigation—crucial elements of the unfolding drama.

The interior of the villa was a blend of luxury and functionality, equipped with advanced security systems.

Every room was designed to facilitate high-level discussions, with a keen eye on safeguarding sensitive information. The choice of this location, away from the bustling city, was deliberate, considering the highly sensitive nature of the case. The villa served as a perfect staging ground for covert operations, where crucial decisions could be made away from the limelight.

Gunang ushered Banjur, the key suspect, into a rounded conference room specifically chosen for the final reveal. The room, circular in design, encouraged a sense of inclusivity yet underlined the gravity of the situation.

The Prime Minister and the Home Minister had taken their places at the main seats of the conference table. Nearby, sat Director Verma, his expression a mix of sternness and expectation. On the other side were a set of other individuals who had connections to this case, their faces a blend of anxiety and defiance as they faced accusations for knowingly or unknowingly aiding the heinous murders.

Ila introduced Banjur as the linchpin of Anup Baruah, the notorious chief of the ATLF. The revelation cast a shadow of grim reality over the room.

Yohan initiated the conversation with Banjur, who had already confessed to the murders. Turning to the Home Minister, Yohan began, "You know how Siddharth was murdered under the guise of a fire breakout in Mumbai, and so was Mekhala."

He then detailed the chilling methodology used in Mekhala's murder, "Banjur received instructions from Anup Baruah to eliminate Mekhala. He discovered that a party was being organised next door at the Bhattacharyas'. By securing a contract there, he found his opportunity."

Yohan meticulously explained the sinister plot, "We found traces of freon in their bodies. The plan was to cause a leak, leading to a fire. But to ensure it reached Mekhala's house and ensured her death, her gas had to be turned on. Banjur, posing as a party organiser from Anand and Surabhi's house, went to Mekhala's under the pretence of borrowing ice, exploiting her trust as a neighbour. Earlier, he had successfully deactivated the CCTV cameras on the floor."

Yohan continued, "Mekhala, unsuspecting and neighbourly, allowed him inside to assist. While Mekhala was fetching the ice, Banjur slyly turned on the gas, leaving it open. He had already instructed the Bhattacharyas' to start heating the party food after 20 minutes, giving him and his team ample time to leave the area. And when Surabhi lit the stove, it was all over. The fire quickly spread to Mekhala's house, engulfing everyone inside."

"But how did Banjur know there was a party at the neighbour's?" the Home Minister asked.

"We'll get to that, sir. But first, let's find out how Samar was murdered and then Zulekha," Ila prayed for patience.

Yohan delved into the details of how Samar, the young Bollywood actor and a key member of the soft power squad, was systematically targeted and eliminated. The *modus operandi* for this murder was decided beforehand. "They had been monitoring Samar ever since they learned he was part of the squad," Yohan began. "Every aspect of his life was under surveillance – his routine, personal life, even his dietary habits. This was going to be their most challenging yet rewarding assassination."

He then explained the lethal method chosen for the murder, "The Chinese military had developed a powerful variant of Fentanyl, a synthetic opioid incredibly potent and lethal in minuscule quantities. Just 2 milligrams, about the size of a few grains of table salt, is enough to kill."

The military ensured that this lethal drug reached the ATLF and Banjur with instructions from Anup Baruah. Banjur and his team waited for the perfect moment to strike.

"During the first wave of COVID-19, Samar went for his vaccine. They couldn't tamper with the vaccine due to tight security, but they observed him closely. After receiving his first COVID-19 vaccine dose, Samar, adhering to protocol, waited for 30 minutes at the centre to monitor for any adverse reactions. This was standard procedure for all vaccinated individuals."

Ila took on from here and continued, "It was during this observation period that Samar developed severe muscle pain in his right hand, a known and common side effect of the vaccine. This detail was crucial for Banjur's plan. After Samar returned home, still in discomfort, he ordered painkillers from a nearby medical store. Due to COVID-19 protocols, the delivery person left the package at the security gate, and one of Samar's staff collected it."

"And that was it! Banjur knew he had to exploit this. He understood the pattern and waited for the right moment to strike. This moment came months later, during Samar's second COVID-19 vaccine dose. Following the same protocol as before, Samar visited the same hospital in Bandra. To Banjur's advantage, Samar again experienced severe pain in his right hand, identical to his reaction after the first dose," Ila summarised.

Yohan detailed how this repetition of events was critical for the execution of the plan. "This consistent reaction provided Banjur with the perfect opportunity. Knowing Samar would likely order the same painkillers again, they prepared to exploit this vulnerability. When the time came, Samar did indeed order the painkillers following his second vaccination dose. Banjur, having anticipated this, had already planted a man at the pharmacy. As soon as Samar's order was placed, the delivery person set out."

The room was silent, hanging on Yohan's every word. "The delivery was made as usual; dropped off at the security gate of Samar's residence. But this was where Banjur's meticulous planning came to fruition. Moments later, Banjur's man, disguised in the same branded T-shirt as the chemist shop's staff, approached the security gate. With a well-rehearsed apology for delivering the wrong package, he swiftly swapped it with another – this one containing the lethal Fentanyl drops and syringe."

Yohan paused, allowing the enormity of the act to sink in, "Unsuspecting and in pain, Samar used the syringe, believing it to be his usual painkiller. It was a normal evening, just another day in his life, until it wasn't. The next day, he was found dead in his room."

The emotional impact of Yohan's words was palpable. "This wasn't just any drug – it was a Chinese variant of Fentanyl, notoriously difficult to trace. During the autopsy, the recent COVID-19 vaccine was identified in his system, leading to no immediate suspicion. It was the perfect crime, masked by the pandemic."

Yohan's voice grew more intense as he delved into the aftermath of Samar's death. "But the ramifications went far beyond a single assassination. Following Samar's death, a well-orchestrated hate campaign was launched against Bollywood. This was part of a larger, carefully planned Chinese agenda to undermine one of India's most influential cultural exports. Bollywood, a symbol of India's soft power, was rapidly gaining popularity in the West and even in China. Samar's death struck a double blow – eliminating a key member of the soft power squad, a cultural ambassador and simultaneously tarnishing the credibility of an entire industry, both domestically and internationally. The Chinese military, through the ATLF, managed to deal a significant blow to India's soft power influence."

As Yohan finished his account, a profound silence enveloped the room, thick with emotion and the weight of his words. The air felt heavy, charged with a sombre realisation of the tragedy that had unfolded. The loss of Samar, a vibrant soul and a cultural icon, resonated as more than just a personal tragedy; it was a calculated strike in a shadowy war of international influence and cultural dominance.

The faces around the room were etched with grief and a deep sense of loss. Samar, who had brought joy and entertainment to millions, whose art transcended borders and cultures, had been reduced to a pawn in a nefarious plot. It was a stark reminder of the cruelty that lay beneath the surface of geopolitical machinations.

In the stillness, the emotional impact of Samar's untimely death was heartbreaking. His absence was not just the loss of a beloved actor but a blow to the collective spirit of a nation that prided itself on its rich cultural heritage. Samar's demise was not just the extinguishing of a life, but an attempt to dim the bright light of India's soft power that shone through its vibrant film industry.

The room, filled with some of the most powerful individuals in the country, was united in a moment of shared mourning. It was a poignant reminder of the human cost of conflict, where cultural ambassadors become targets and art becomes a battleground. The story of Samar, his life and his tragic end would remain etched in their memories, a sombre testament to the darker aspects of international relations and cultural warfare.

With a heavy heart, the Home Minister broke the silence that had enveloped the room. "We lost one of our best," he said solemnly, his eyes lingering on a specific person in the room.

"Absolutely, sir," Ila echoed, her voice unusually tinged with emotion, a rare crack in her typically composed exterior.

Yohan, feeling the weight of the moment but understanding the urgency of their mission, continued, "Sir, let's now turn to Zulekha's murder, which involved the same lethal substance."

The Prime Minister, puzzled, interjected, "But how's that possible? She died in 2019 before COVID was even a concern in India."

"Yes, sir, the same substance, but a different strategy," Yohan confirmed, and with a nod towards Gunang, he invited her to reveal the details. "Gunang, please share what you've found."

Gunang, initially taken aback by her sudden inclusion, felt a rush of adrenaline. She was new to the team and had been kept on the sidelines at the Prime Minister's office. Now, she was thrust into the spotlight, given the chance of a lifetime to present in front of the nation's most influential figures. She could feel her eyes well up with gratitude. Sensing her initial hesitation, Yohan gave her an encouraging pat on the back, whispering, "You got this, Gunang. Make it quick; we have much to uncover."

Collecting her thoughts and emotions, Gunang began, her voice steady but charged with the significance of her words, "Sir, as you may recall, Zulekha was found dead under mysterious circumstances in her hotel room in Delhi. She was the first victim in this series of murders. She had flown down to Delhi to meet Mekhala and share crucial findings. Recognising the immediate threat she posed with her knowledge, Banjur's team needed to act fast.

"Their method was simple yet effective. They poisoned her soup with drops of Fentanyl, delivered straight to her room. It was a silent kill – no physical assault, no forced entry, no suicide note. Everything was designed to leave no trace, no reason for suspicion. They exploited the fact that autopsies are typically conducted soon after death, while

Fentanyl takes weeks to manifest in the body. Thus, her death appeared to be from natural causes, not warranting further investigation, as she had no known enemies. This murder served as a test to assess whether the lethal drug could be traced before using it on higher-profile targets like Samar."

Gunang concluded, and a hush fell over the room. The cunning and ruthlessness of the murderers were starkly evident, each detail underscoring the cold calculation behind these heinous crimes. The revelations painted a disturbing picture of a meticulously planned operation, leaving everyone in the room grappling with the extent of the conspiracy they were uncovering.

***

The Prime Minister, leaning forward with a newfound respect in his eyes, addressed the CBI team directly. "Yohan. Team. Good job on uncovering the murders." His deliberate use of Yohan's first name, rather than the more formal 'Tytler', signified a rising fondness and a recognition of his capabilities, a subtle nod to the officer's commendable work.

"But there are so many questions left unanswered," the Prime Minister continued, his tone reflecting both appreciation and the urgency to delve deeper. "Why was Zulekha the first to be targeted? What exactly did she find out that made her such a threat? Why did she leave Assam years before and relocate? And most importantly," he paused, the weight of his next question hanging in the air, "Have you nabbed the mastermind behind all this – Anup Baruah?"

"We'll answer all your questions, sir. Let's start with what Zulekha discovered that triggered this series of killings." Realising the importance of detailing Zulekha's background and movements, Yohan circled back to a crucial point in her story, "It was around 2018 when she decided to base herself in Shillong, working there as a journalist. It wasn't just a random choice. She was playing it smart, staying under the radar to avoid suspicion by moving from Assam for a while."

He glanced around the room, ensuring he had everyone's attention, "While she was based in Shillong, her heart and mission were still deeply entrenched in Assam. She would frequently travel there, skilfully juggling her roles as a journalist and a part-time yoga instructor."

Yohan's expression showed a mix of admiration and solemnity as he spoke about Zulekha. "You see, her articles were tactfully crafted. They weren't screaming headlines about the ATLF, but more subtle, thought-provoking pieces targeting an audience of young, English-speaking school and college students. And her yoga classes? She taught exclusively women in the area, using yoga not only as a tool for physical and mental well-being but also as a subtle means of cultural infiltration. Through her yoga classes, she spread the essence of India's rich culture. The idea was to instil a sense of national pride and identity, especially among the women, who in turn would influence their families and communities."

He paused, letting the significance of Zulekha's work sink in, "When her influence started gaining momentum, Zulekha did the unexpected. She stepped back and moved away from Assam. A tough call, but necessary for her safety. Yet, she never really disconnected. She kept tabs on the region, especially the youngsters she had interacted with."

Yohan's voice took on a more serious tone, "And that's when she hit upon something alarming. Zulekha, in her routine comings and goings, started picking up on a peculiar pattern in Assam, something that didn't quite add up."

He paused for effect, making sure he had the full attention of the room, "She noticed that an increasing number of students, especially from the villages she had been focusing on, were heading abroad for education. And not just anywhere – specifically to China. These were bright kids, but they weren't making it through the competitive exams despite coaching. Barriers, you know, the kind that many from such areas face."

Yohan's tone grew more serious. "This sudden spike in students moving to China set off alarm bells for Zulekha. She knew she had stumbled onto something big, something potentially sinister. Diving deeper, she discovered most of these students were from the same coaching centre – Brighter Tutorials in Tinsukia."

He gestured with his hands to emphasise his point. "Zulekha shared this with Siddharth, who focused on education. Siddharth was quick to realise the gravity of this trend. He suggested Zulekha get inside Brighter Tutorials, preferably their headquarters, to unearth what was really going on. Taking this advice, she managed to land a job at Brighter Tutorials. It was the turning point that led her into the heart of what we now know was a much larger, more complex operation."

"How are they involved?" the Home Minister inquired, seeking clarity.

Yohan turned towards Ila, signalling her to take the lead. Her reputation for being straightforward and incisive made her the ideal person to explain the complexities of the case.

Ila stepped forward, her demeanour reflecting her characteristic directness. "That brings us to the next culprit, sir," she said, gesturing to the police officers. The officers escorted in a tall man, still dressed in his business suit from his arrest, handcuffed.

Ila, with a tone of steely resolve, introduced him. Sirs, this is Bill Charles, the CEO of Brighter Tutorials," she began, pointing towards the handcuffed figure. "He was systematically being paid to share data about students from

Assam and other bordering states, particularly those who couldn't clear their exams."

She continued, delving into the financial irregularities that had raised red flags during their investigation. "We uncovered numerous inconsistencies in Bill's financial assets, which led us to suspect his involvement. It appears that Banjur was the liaison, the point person who accessed all this data and then passed it on to Anup Baruah."

"The tactics used were manipulative," Ila added. "They lured students into joining prestigious institutes in China, offering them education at a fraction of the usual cost and promising a brighter future. This was the information Zulekha was digging into. She even managed to make contact with some of the students and their families."

Ila's voice took on a tone of disdain as she described Bill's complicity. "Bill was fully aware of the murky waters he was treading in, yet he continued to supply this crucial data to Banjur and, through him, to the ATLF. All for what? Just money."

Bill stood there as Ila concluded her briefing, his head hanging low in shame. The Home Minister, visibly appalled by the betrayal, lashed out, "Shame on you, mister. You were selling out your country for what... money? You were a well-compensated CEO, and yet you chose greed."

The Prime Minister, who had been listening intently, chimed in with a pressing question, reflective of his analytical mind. "But this doesn't add up, Ila. I understand Bill's motive was financial. But what does Anup Baruah gain from sending these kids to Chinese institutes?"

Yohan, confident and smiling, stepped forward, "That's precisely the question we wanted you to ask, sir." He glanced meaningfully at the Prime Minister, "What Zulekha uncovered next was indeed shocking. But before I get to that, let me highlight another related aspect that helped us nab these culprits."

He turned to the Home Minister, his expression serious, "Remember, sir, we mentioned that Mekhala's husband, Adinarayan, was the one who leaked information to the media about our investigation into Zulekha? We arrested him in Assam, and he revealed something crucial. The big question was, how did Adinarayan find out about our investigation? The obvious answer is that someone tipped him off. But who made that mistake… a rather overconfident one?"

***

"Sir, you asked the most important question. What does Anup Baruah gain from all this?" Yohan began, his voice steady, signalling their investigation's final, crucial reveal.

Just as Yohan was about to continue, Ila interjected with a dramatic twist. "But before that, let's address another mystery. The person who tipped Adinarayan about Zulekha early on is right here, in this very room." Her statement sent a ripple of shock across the room.

Yohan and Ila exchanged a knowing look, a faint smile hinting at the magnitude of the revelation they were about to make. "Sirs, his presence among us would normally raise suspicion," Yohan said, his tone suggesting the irony of the situation.

He walked confidently towards the other end of the conference room, where Adinarayan was seated. The room's attention followed his every step, and the atmosphere charged with anticipation. Stopping right next to Adinarayan, Yohan stood behind a man seated there. "This," he said, turning to face the ministers, "is the man who tipped Adinarayan about the Zulekha angle."

The ministers and everyone else in the room were visibly stunned. Disbelief and shock were written on their faces as they struggled to comprehend the revelation. The man in question, the informant, was a familiar face to all.

With a calm demeanour, Ila approached the man and gently patted his back, "But don't worry, sir. There is some relief for you in all of this." The man she stood beside was none other than Kailash Mukherjee, the leader of the opposition. He was the one who had vehemently criticised the investigation, even going so far as to accuse the Prime Minister himself.

"Why give him any relief at all?" the HM lashed out, looking at Kailash.

"Because, sir. Much like Banjur, he, too, was a pawn in the larger scheme of things. In his case, Kailash *ji* didn't even know that he was a part of this crime".

"What do you mean?" the PM asked.

"Sir, to fully grasp the situation, we need to unravel the final piece of the puzzle. What exactly did Zulekha find?" Ila posed the crucial question, her tone indicating that they were on the brink of a major breakthrough.

Yohan took over, "The connection of Brighter Tutorials funnelling students to China had Zulekha on edge. She knew there was more to it. She had watched interviews of Anup Baruah and was convinced that he wasn't working alone and lacked the intellect to mastermind this operation by himself. While Zulekha was digging into Brighter Tutorials, she passed her findings to Mekhala, who stumbled upon another critical angle."

Ila chimed in, "Do you recall, sirs, us mentioning one of Mekhala's authors, Mukut Apang?" The Home Minister nodded, indicating his recollection of the name.

Yohan continued, "Mukut Apang had unearthed a financial scam of significant proportions. During the COVID pandemic, new loan apps like Panda Cash, QwikRupee, and RupeeInstant were disbursing loans to Indians during the financial crisis. These apps were controlled by a powerful individual."

He paused for a moment, letting the information sink in, "This man was collecting data on all these financially vulnerable people. The information was then passed to Banjur, who, in turn, relayed it to Anup Baruah. The sinister plan was to lure these individuals with easy and instant loans. But when they couldn't repay, they were coerced into completing 'tasks' or 'chores', effectively turning them into agents for orchestrating a series of attacks within India."

Ila added, "If caught, these individuals wouldn't reveal anything. The secrecy in exchange for their debts being written off. The safety of their families from financial ruin ensured their silence."

The room was gripped by the chilling nature of the reveal. The implication that a financial scam was a front for recruiting unwilling agents to carry out attacks on Indian soil was not just shocking but also a testament to the depth and cunning of the conspiracy they were uncovering.

"How did Mukut uncover this?" the Home Minister asked, leaning forward with keen interest.

With a tone of analytical precision, Ila replied, "Mukut's initial story was focused on the ease of access to loans and their security concerns. But it was Mekhala who dug deeper, uncovering a crucial link - all these loan apps had Chinese investors."

Yohan added, "Mekhala, realising the gravity of this information, decided to counteract it. She commissioned a book discussing how China was manipulating education and finance to turn Indians against their own country. This book, authored by MR Shaikh, was set to be adapted into a film starring Samar. The idea was to keep the book's content subtle enough to avoid alerting those being investigated. That is why she never commissioned the book to any publisher and encouraged Mr. Shaikh to self-publish it. She told him she could secure a film deal for him if he did so. Mekhala knew that the book should be kept low-key and focus more on the film. After all, a film, thanks to its wider audience and the involvement of a major star like Samar, would give the issue a much higher reach."

Ila nodded towards the police, signalling them. "Bring him in," she commanded. The room's attention shifted as another figure, a familiar face from earlier in the investigation, was brought in, handcuffed and made to stand next to Banjur and Bill Charles. "Meet Himanta Barua, the supposed owner of these loan apps. In reality, he's just a front, a *benami*, for his Chinese investors."

The room's atmosphere intensified with this revelation. Here was a plot that used the most unassuming means - education and financial aid - to orchestrate a covert war against India. The notion that such commonplace elements of daily life were being weaponised in a new form of warfare was chilling.

Yohan observed the room, "This shocking plan wasn't just about individual acts of espionage or sabotage. It was an attempt to infiltrate and influence the very fabric of our society – targeting our youth through education and preying on the vulnerable through financial schemes. It was a silent war that, if left unchecked, could have far-reaching effects, challenging the integrity and sovereignty of India."

The collective realisation of the extent and depth of this conspiracy left everyone in the room with a profound sense of the threat they were facing. It wasn't just a matter of National security; it was about protecting the core values and stability of the Nation.

*****

As the Home Minister pondered over the identities of the key players, he questioned, "So, who among these is the mastermind?"

With a knowing smirk, Yohan replied, "Oh, these are all soldiers, sir. The true mastermind would be someone more influential, someone in a position of power, close to the corridors of power to execute all these."

"And that is Anup Baruah?" the HM asked, seeking confirmation.

"I am getting to that, sir," Yohan continued with a focused tone. "So, after commissioning the book, Mekhala received a tip from a source in InfoEdge Analytics about the ATLF's interest in using AhaLife's data for their election campaign. Mekhala then contacted Zulekha and instructed her to start working as a yoga influencer on the app from Assam to see if she would be approached for any related campaign. Meanwhile, Mekhala closely monitored the findings through George Alfred, the author, and his source."

The Home Minister, intrigued by the unfolding details, asked, "And was AhaLife involved in this too?"

"They might have been," Yohan replied thoughtfully. "In fact, we met their CEO, Anirban. He informed us that the deal didn't go through because he had a specific condition for proceeding. Had the deal been successful, he might not have disclosed this to us. But since it fell through, he candidly shared the one reason that caused the deal's failure."

"And what was that?" Arvind inquired, his interest clearly piqued by the new information.

Yohan nodded, ready to unveil the final chapter of their investigation. "For that, I need to tell you a story, sir. The final piece of this intricate puzzle is what Zulekha discovered, and that changed everything.

"Zulekha's journey to uncover Anup Baruah's true intentions was exhaustive and meticulous. She began by visiting the homes of children who had been persuaded to study in China. But when that didn't yield concrete results, she delved deeper into Baruah's past, his family, and extended network. Guised as a journalist, she travelled to Tinsukia, claiming she wanted to portray Anup and the ATLF's side of the story.

"Her investigation into Baruah's life revealed small yet telling details. Despite his notoriety, he still funded his village school and contributed to community facilities. Secret visits to attend weddings, name newborn children, and participate in local functions were part of his routine. The people in his village greatly benefited from his contributions, and it helped in maintaining a positive image. However, Zulekha noticed a significant change in 2019. While Baruah's financial support continued, his physical presence in the village had ceased. For over 18 months, no one had seen him there, a stark departure from his previous frequent visits. Instead, he maintained his presence through virtual means, sending recorded messages and speeches to stay connected.

"Indeed, Zulekha's thorough investigation led her to the local library in Tinsukia, where she found a treasure trove of information. The library had archived several of Anup Baruah's recorded meetings and speeches, a resource that proved invaluable for her research.

Zulekha spent countless hours in the library, poring over these recordings. She watched and rewatched them, attentive to every detail, every nuance in Baruah's speech and demeanour. It was during this meticulous review that she noticed Baruah's consistent habit of moving his wrists while speaking.

"This particular mannerism, which at first seemed trivial, turned out to be a crucial clue. Zulekha cross-referenced this observation with other available footage of Baruah, including the sole interview he had given to Adinarayan early in his career and some old YouTube videos. In each instance, this unique gesture was evident, almost like a signature trait of Baruah. This small, seemingly inconsequential detail caught Zulekha's attention and led her to a groundbreaking hypothesis."

Sensing the heightened suspense in the room, Yohan prepared to deliver the most shocking revelation of their investigation. "What if Anup Baruah didn't exist in the form as we knew him?" he posited, his words hanging in the air like a bombshell.

The Home Minister, perplexed and intrigued, leaned in. "What does that mean?" he asked, his brows furrowed in confusion.

With a slight hint of dramatic flair, Yohan explained, "In this era of AI and technology, recreating a dead person's imagery isn't as far-fetched as it seems. All you need are reference videos, audio clips, and other intricate details."

A collective sigh, tinged with despair and disbelief, echoed through the room, even affecting the likes of Adinarayan and Kailash Mukherjee.

"Dead… dead. What do you mean?" Kailash stuttered, his voice betraying his shock.

Yohan continued; the intensity in his voice rising, "What I mean is that Zulekha's most important discovery was that Anup Baruah was no more. Someone has been using his identity, not just to manipulate the ATLF and its operatives like Banjur but also to wage a cultural and information warfare against our country."

The room fell into stunned silence, the weight of Yohan's revelation dawning on everyone present. The thought that the Anup Baruah they had been chasing, the mastermind they believed was orchestrating this complex plot, was long dead and his identity hijacked for nefarious purposes was shocking and unsettling.

The implications of this discovery were enormous – it meant that the entire operation was even more sophisticated and deceptive than they had initially thought. The person or people behind this ruse had not only successfully manipulated the ATLF but had also managed to keep up the facade of a living, influential leader to further their sinister agenda. The revelation added a new, chilling dimension to the case, indicating a level of technological manipulation and strategic planning that was unprecedented and deeply alarming.

The tension in the room heightened as the Home Minister's questions hung in the air, "Then who has been sending instructions to Banjur? Who was Banjur sending the data to? Who is behind all this?" he demanded.

With a deliberate and theatrical pace, Yohan walked around the room, his steps echoing slightly on the polished floor. The eyes of every person present followed him, sensing that a critical moment was about to unfold. He stopped purposefully behind one person. "Remember, I said the mastermind had to be someone close to the corridors of power?" Yohan remarked, his voice tinged with a hint of revelation.

The ministers and everyone else in the room strained their necks to see where Yohan had positioned himself. The sight that met their eyes was startling. Yohan was standing right behind Kailash Mukherjee, the leader of the opposition. Mukherjee, visibly sweating, seemed to shrink under the weight of Yohan's proximity and the implications it carried.

"Kailash *ji*, you gave information on Zulekha to Adinarayan," Yohan stated, his gaze fixed on Mukherjee. "Remember how you got that information. Something to think about," he then signalled to the policemen, "Bring him in."

The room's atmosphere turned electric as the door opened slowly. In walked a man, impeccably dressed in formal attire from his shirt to shoes, handcuffed and escorted by policemen. His eyes, locked with Yohan's, betrayed no despair or defeat but rather a readiness to confront whatever lay ahead.

"This, ladies and gentlemen, is Anup Baruah, or rather, the man who kept that legacy alive," Ila announced, her voice steady but carrying the weight of the revelation.

Not taking his eyes off Mukherjee, Yohan added, "Now you know why you are responsible, ah, Kailash *ji*?" The leader of the opposition looked incredulous, his eyes widening in disbelief at the man who stood before him.

"Kailash *ji*," Yohan continued, his tone slightly mocking, "... would you care to introduce the mastermind of this conspiracy to everyone present? The man who managed to fool even you, a politician known for his acumen and intelligence."

The room was now a whirlpool of emotions – shock, disbelief, and the realisation of the depth of deception they had all been subjected to. The mastermind of the entire operation, the man they believed to be Anup Baruah, stood handcuffed, a symbol of the intricate web of lies and manipulation that had ensnared them all. The revelation that even Kailash Mukherjee, a seasoned politician, had been duped added a dramatic twist to the already complex narrative.

The room was engulfed in intense suspense as Kailash Mukherjee, his usual strong and confident demeanour faltering, identified the man before them, "This... this is my PA, Anthony... Anthony Raju," his voice dropped, reflecting his disbelief and shock.

With a hint of irony in his tone, Yohan corrected him, "Well, that's what he told you… or rather, the story he concocted about himself. The touching tale of Anthony Raju from Nagaland, a simple yet brilliant strategist. Quite a narrative, wasn't it?" He gazed at the man known as Anthony with a scrutinising eye.

The mastermind retorted defiantly, "Your most brilliant people were fooled, officer."

Yohan, unfazed, replied coolly, "Hmm. But eventually caught. Right, Mr. Jonathan Wang? That's his real name, Kailash *ji*." He then unravelled the true identity and background of the mastermind, "Jonathan was a trained operative under the Chinese military, who infiltrated into India during the Commonwealth Games in 2010. He spent years in Kolkata's Chinatown, absorbing Indian characteristics, while his backstory as a Nagaland native was crafted. Being from a conflict-ridden area made it easier to weave his fictional rise through the academic ranks."

Yohan continued, detailing Jonathan's meticulously built identity. "They needed a believable identity, and they found one in Anthony Raju from Nagaland, whose family died in a train accident. His degrees from Harvard and Singapore were all part of the elaborate ruse. Yohan, with a flair for striking when the iron is hot, expanded on the crucial turning point that led to Jonathan Wang's infiltration into the Indian political landscape. "Let's consider the political backdrop that facilitated Jonathan's entry," he began, ensuring everyone in the room grasped the full context.

"It was 2016, a critical time for Kailash Mukherjee's party, especially in the Northeast. They were losing their grip on the states there, one by one. It was a significant setback, and for a politician like Kailash *ji*, holding onto power and influence in that region was imperative.

Yohan's tone underscored the strategic political manoeuvring at play. "In a bid to strengthen his party's position and connect with the Northeastern electorate, Kailash *ji* decided to bring someone from the region into his inner circle. He specifically wanted a PA from one of the seven sister states, someone who could add credibility to his commitment to the Northeast."

He paused, letting the significance of this decision sink in. "Enter Jonathan Wang, posing as Anthony Raju from Nagaland. With his fabricated backstory of a brilliant but humble upbringing, coupled with his fake credentials from prestigious universities, he was the perfect candidate. For a man of Jonathan's calculative intellect, it wasn't difficult to secure the position. He fit the bill perfectly – a seemingly brilliant strategist from Nagaland with impressive academic credentials."

Yohan walked a few steps, gesturing to emphasise his point. "That position as Kailash *ji's* PA was Jonathan's golden ticket. It placed him right next to the corridors of power, giving him access, influence, and, most importantly, the cover to orchestrate his plans. He was hiding in plain sight, leveraging his proximity to power while covertly pulling the strings as Anup Baruah. After all, his military had eliminated Anup when he visited China, and now his identity was passed on to Jonathan or Anthony."

"But you know, it's often the smallest slip that unravels the most intricate of plans," he said with satisfaction and disbelief. "One… rather two silly mistakes that cost him everything. He thought he was being clever, trying to misdirect us towards Adinarayan. So he slipped the information about us investigating Zulekha to Kailash *ji*, who in turn passed it to Mr. Adinarayan."

He paced a few steps, the suspense in the room building with each word. "The moment Adinarayan mentioned his source, a lightbulb went off in our heads. That was the breakthrough we needed," Yohan gestured emphatically, his eyes scanning the room, making sure everyone grasped the significance of this revelation.

"The other mistake was the disappearance of George Alfred. His revelations were more concerning for the ATLF than for AhaLife, given the potential impact of the author's book. Anirban revealed to us that the deal didn't go through because he had one condition... a face-to-face meeting with Anup Baruah," Ila added, further clarifying the situation. "Jonathan, posing as Anup, declined this request over a call. Consequently, Anirban had no real motive to kidnap George. It was Jonathan who planned the kidnapping, and Banjur executed it. Jonathan probably thought that if an investigation ever took place, we would be misdirected towards AhaLife. Not a very smart move to make," Ila concluded, highlighting the oversight in Jonathan's plan.

"Anyways, once we found that Adinarayan got the tip from Kailash *ji*, we started zeroing in on all his close contacts. Piece by piece, connection by connection, we began to peel away the layers of deceit. And what did we find?" Yohan paused for a moment, letting the suspense hang in the air.

"Underneath it all was his criminal mask. The mastermind, the puppeteer behind this entire charade, was right there, hiding in plain sight," Yohan's voice resonated with a mix of triumph and incredulity.

He exhaled deeply, the weight of the investigation's culmination evident in his demeanour. "Phew," he breathed out, almost in relief, as he concluded his findings. The revelation marked not just the end of a complex investigation but also showcased the cunning and depth of international espionage and its ability to infiltrate and manipulate at the highest levels.

As the intensity of the revelations reached its climax, Yohan turned decisively towards the officers present in the room. His firm and resolute voice carried the weight of justice about to be served. "Take him, officers. Put this son of a… behind bars. We've only just begun to uncover the depths of his country's deceit," he declared, his tone a blend of satisfaction and resolve.

This moment marked a significant victory for Yohan, a culmination of tireless effort and unwavering determination in solving one of the most convoluted cases of his career. His gaze swept across the room, landing on Ila, Gunang, and Director Verma. Their faces mirrored his own sense of accomplishment and relief, a shared recognition of the arduous journey they had embarked on together.

Yet, amidst this triumph, Yohan's thoughts drifted to Sukumar, his comrade-in-arms, still in the hospital fighting to recover. His eyes, brimming with a mix of triumph and sorrow, briefly closed as he paid silent homage to his teammate, his brother in arms. The bittersweet moment underscored the sacrifices and personal costs that often accompanied their duty to uncover the truth and uphold justice.

***

The Prime Minister's expression of relief and satisfaction was evident as he commended the team, "Good job, Verma. Great stuff, Yohan, Ila, and… what is your name, child?" his attention turned to the youngest member of the team.

"It's Gunang, sir," she replied with a confidence that belied her inexperience.

The PM's smile broadened, a gesture of appreciation and encouragement. He then pulled Yohan aside, a gesture that revealed a comfortable familiarity. Yohan, slightly taken aback but pleased, returned the smile.

"So, what plans now, young man? Going for a break?" the Prime Minister inquired.

"Yes, sir," Yohan replied, his thoughts already turning to his next steps.

"Where to?" probed the PM.

"Not anywhere specific, sir. I just want to be there to help Sukumar recover. He may not have been here today, but this case is as much his victory as anybody else's on this team."

The Prime Minister nodded, "Oh, he will be fine, Yohan. Be with him."

"Yes, sir," Yohan acknowledged.

"But I want you to come back soon," the PM added, his tone turning slightly more serious.

Yohan's expression shifted to one of curiosity. "What happened, sir?"

The Prime Minister explained, "There's another case, and I need you to work on that. You'll have to go to Hyderabad."

The mention of Hyderabad stirred a flood of fond memories in Yohan's mind. He had spent part of his childhood there with his father and late mother. Pushing aside the nostalgia, he focused on the present. "What is this case, sir?"

"I'll pass the details to Verma," the PM assured. Then, with a pause that hinted at something deeper, he added, "There's one small thing, Yohan."

The officer stood attentively, "What is it, sir?"

"Well, unlike your last two cases, this one might get personal for you at some point. And at that moment, I want you to remember why you chose this profession and not your dad's." With those cryptic words, the Prime Minister walked away.

Yohan stood there with a myriad of emotions and thoughts swirling in his mind. The PM's words hinted at unknown challenges and personal connections yet to be uncovered. "To new challenges," he whispered to himself, ready to embark on the next journey, armed with the experience of the past and the uncertainty of what lay ahead.

NOBODY LIKES AN OUTSIDER IN THE MEDIA

Perfect blend of mystery, suspense, thriller, and politics.
Times of India

A stellar debut novel with a raw flavour of Indian politics and murder investigation.
The New Indian Express

This book promises to have you on the edge of your seat.
The Daily Guardian

True to his title, Fawaz Jaleel's writing makes him an outsider too. The narratives aren't forced and don't shy away from expressing what exists in reality. This approach is probably what makes 'Nobody Likes An Outsider' stand out from similar crime/thriller and political thriller books
Asianet

The depth in research, seamless mix of fiction and non-fiction, and keeping the mystery alive till the end along with non-preachy socio-political commentary puts Fawaz Jaleel among one of the finest Indian thriller authors.
The Sunday Guardian

As one of India's best-selling authors, Jaleel's work stands as a testament to his skillful storytelling and deep understanding of India's political and social dynamics
The Weekly Mail

NOBODY LIKES AN OUTSIDER
READER REVIEWS

(If you have written a review for this book on Amazon/Flipkart/Goodreads/Google/Blog etc., please share a screenshot to fawazjr@gmail.com and we'll be happy to feature it in the coming editions)

Murder mystery with brutal truth of society- Srijoni Chakraborty

Books that uphold the reality of society and speak what most of us are urged to but can't due to helplessness, should be credited separately. I liked everything about this book starting from the plot to the climax, to character development, to the portrayal. Hope to read more rebel books fiercely protesting against unlawfulness, communalism, religious conflict, and the ugly usage of the power of so-called influential people

Absolute Thriller - Dharmendra

With a very intriguing plot and characters, Author Fawaz Jaleel has woven an edge-of-the-seat thriller. The book not only dishes out an entertaining story but also sheds light on some of the crucial issues of Indian politics. Overall, it's a promising book with lots of nuances. I won't be surprised if it is adapted into a web series or movie. Highly recommended!

Unexpected Climax - Kiruthiga Shankar Kumar

It's a treat for all thriller lovers. There were many suspects, but the final reveal was shocking 😲.

Nice Book - Gaurav Ghosh

After a long time, I found a book that rekindled my interest. I couldn't stop myself from falling into its trap, and the result was clear: swollen eyes and a satisfied mind after a sleepless night. Gripping plot, lucid description, and creative juxtaposition of the political landscape with the narrative... This one is a compelling read!

FAWAZ JALEEL

Fawaz Jaleel is an Indian author and columnist known for his crime thrillers and murder mysteries. His debut novel, "Nobody Likes An Outsider," is a national bestseller and is being adapted into a Hindi motion picture. Previously, he served as a consultant to the Government of India on a project managed by the Prime Minister's office, MyGov India. He collaborated with senior bureaucrats and government members on several projects, including PM Modi's first Townhall in India. His other works include three short stories: "From the Land of Palaces," "The Legend of Birbal's Bull," and "Inspiring Indians."

Before this, Fawaz was associated with companies like OPEN, UpGrad, NDTV, and NIUM. He began his career in Public Health, working on projects with UNAIDS, USAID, the Government of India, and The Global Fund. He earned his Bachelor's in Journalism from Madras Christian College and his Master's in Development from Azim Premji University.

Follow him on instagram - @fawazsays or write to him at fawazjr@gmail.com